Byou

Cho

My Life as an Architect in Seoul

CONTENTS

INTRODUCTION

My life as an architect in Seoul has been a happy journey, one of exploration with the same natural curiosity I had as a child. Seoul is where I was born and raised, and where I lived until moving abroad to study architecture in the early 1980s. When I was young, I would walk long distances to school every day, and encounter old men playing traditional board games like *jangi* or *go* and women gathering on street corners to gossip. I still carry these peaceful moments with me in my heart, and they fill me with happiness and contentment.

In the 1960s and '70s, Seoul was a small and relatively quiet city, with only a few cars and even fewer tall buildings. The first transportation I ever took was an electric-powered tram with wooden seats and windows. I still remember trying to catch a glimpse of the city as it rushed past, fascinated by the ever-changing scenery.

When I returned to Seoul in the early 1990s, after living in Europe and the US for nearly ten years, I found the streets bursting with people, cars, modern buildings and motorways like 99 Olympic-ro and Gangbyeon-ro. I noticed that the Gangnam area south of the river in particular had become populated with new buildings and even more cars! Many of my friends, also architects, rushed to move there. It was starting to be seen as being better designed – an artificial, manmade section of the city with plenty of scope for opportunities in the future. I also decided to move my office to Gangnam, and began working on projects in the area.

People often ask what I think about the rapid change and growth of Seoul over the last few decades, usually expecting me to be in favour of these modern developments. In my view, however, the old parts of the city – clustered around the foothills of the mountains, leading up narrow alleyways to groups of compact houses, huddled together – were much more attractive. I am very happy that I have my painting studio, gallery and music bar (see p. 47), where my friends can drop in at any time. It is located in Seochon in the old part of Seoul, surrounded by palaces, *hanoks* (small, traditional houses) and narrow, winding lanes.

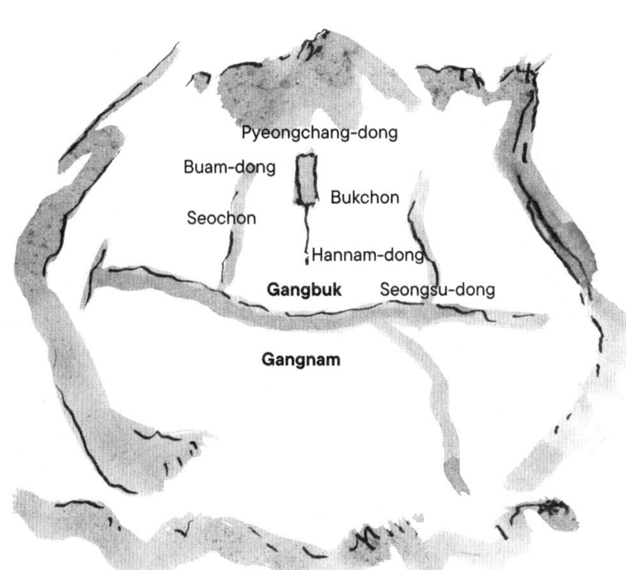

GANGBUK

The term 'Gangbuk' describes broadly the area north of the Han River, which formed the whole of the city until it expanded to the south. At the turn of the 20th century, Seoul was more like a series of villages, with strong connections to its rural surroundings. Unlike Paris or London, it had no buildings over a single storey in height, apart from the royal palaces. The cityscape was instead defined by its topography, which dictated a natural hierarchy.

Seoul underwent several dramatic changes and periods of destruction and rebuilding at various times in its history, including Japanese Colonial rule (1910–45), the Korean War (1950–53) and the rapid economic developments that took place from the 1960s to the 1980s, influenced by the American dream of a modern city of highrise buildings connected by highways. The mayor at the time, Kim Hyun-ok, set out to replace Seoul's old neighbourhoods with large, contemporary buildings. Overpasses were built across rivers, and trees that once lined boulevards were uprooted to add more lanes. I grew up with the construction of heavy infrastructure happening everywhere around me.

Yet Seoul is not only a product of these recent changes, but also a masterpiece of late 14th-century architectural planning. Some areas in the north of the city still remind me of the Seoul of my childhood. These neighbourhoods, huddled along narrow alleyways, retain some aspects of the old city. In my own art and architecture, I can still vividly feel the values of beauty I have preserved from my childhood. The peaceful streets lined

The typical *hanok* interior of Buam House, with folding paper doors and soy-oil paper on the floor. The floor catches the light and creates a distinctive ambience in the space.

with *hanoks* where I grew up gave me many opportunities for exploring my surroundings and observing the people who lived there.

As a child, I was fascinated by the sensory experience of rain: the particular smell after a rain shower, how the sky closed and opened up again, and the interplay of light and shadow. I can remember falling asleep to shadows dancing across the paper windows on windy nights, the soft glow of the moonlight on my walls and how the passage of weeks was defined by the phases of the moon. Eventually, I would give in to the darkness, before being awakened by the golden hues of the morning sun.

These memories have been an important contribution to my architectural process, especially when designing in the neighbourhoods of Bukchon (p. 26) and Seochon (p. 34). When spending time in these areas, it is easier to understand why light is rarely spoken about in isolation. It is bound to forces such as temperature and humidity, and positive and negative space. This may be due to the Korean climate, or perhaps to the design of the *hanok*, which opens onto a courtyard with just a single, thin layer of paper (*hanji*) separating the interior space from the outside.

Heavy humidity dominates in spring and summer, and creates a softened light, inextricable from fog. During autumn and winter, following the monsoon season, the light becomes clear and cold, and the colours more intensely vibrant. At this time of year, the leaves of the tall ginkgo tree (*Eunhaeng namu*), so typical of this region, change from green to bright yellow.

The architecture acts as a mediator, connecting humans with the natural world, rather than shielding them from it. In the *hanoks* that can still be found along the small alleyways, almost all of the rooms are oriented towards the outside. They are I- or L-shaped in plan, without hallways or foyers. Alcoves do not exist, and rooms flow into one another. I grew up in one of these traditional houses, perhaps the reason why I am so interested in how light and shadow are perceived, as well as in how nature finds its way into a building.

Over the centuries, *hanoks* have been designed with particular attention paid to how the buildings are positioned in relation to their setting, with the focus on landscape and seasons. Ideally, a *hanok* would be placed with the river at the front and the mountains at the back. Local building materials would be used, including earth, rocks, timber and *hanji*. This approach can be traced back to the original urban planning of Hanyang (the old name of Seoul) in the late 14th century, a city that was laid out according to several topographic and climatic parameters.

In the north, Seoul is sheltered from the cold winter winds by mountains: Bukaksan (*buk* means 'north', *ak* is 'rocky' and *san* 'mountain') and Bukhansan (*han* refers to the Han River). In the summer, a cool breeze from the south passes over open fields and rivers, and in the evening cold air floats down the foothills north of Seoul. The infrastructure and streets follow the direction of the streams and channels of the Han River. Seoul was an early example of a sustainably planned city, laid out deliberately to benefit from the climatic and geographic conditions, including fresh breezes to improve air quality.

Map of Seoul from 1825, with mountains to the north and the river shown as a thick line at the south and west.

Its location in the foothills protected it from river floods in summer and provided potential connections for transport and supplies of food and water. Korean town planning has traditionally understood that working with nature is more beneficial than trying to control it. As soon as dams around rivers or long, wide roads that carve up the landscape begin to appear, there will be negative consequences.

Preserving regional heritage and the natural flow of the landscape is crucial to successful continuous urban planning. This is why the roads and buildings follow the lines dictated by nature and preserve a certain scale; you will not find wide roads stretching from east to west or south to north in a traditional Korean village. This principle remains in some hidden places of Seoul, especially in Bukchon, Seochon and Insa-dong, also in the north. When I find myself in these areas today, I am transported back to the days when I wandered along the narrow, organically meandering alleyways, listening to people chatting, smelling the food being cooked in their homes and watching the interplay of light and shadow on the ground and the walls.

The architect Kim Swoo-geun (1931–1986), as well as contemporary architects like Inchul Kim, Min Hyun-sik and Seung H-Sang, have all responded to this unique character in the old fabric of the city. Kim Swoo-geun, who paved the way for Korea's modern architecture, built many beautifully executed projects that emphasized the value of small alleyways, a human scale and the sequential experience of places, which can still be found in parts of Gangbuk. I still remember Kim's famous phrase: 'The better the street: the narrower, the better; the worse the street: the wider, the better.'

Space Group Building (1971), designed by Kim Swoo-geun, breaks down a large mass into smaller segments. Inside, this fragmentation can be experienced as you are led through spaces of varying sizes. These spatial and progressional considerations are even more vividly and clearly evident in his Kyungdong Presbyterian Church (1980). By placing the entrance at the far end of the building, Kim provided an opportunity for visitors to gather and socialize after the service. It also works as a sound barrier between the street and the church. This large, monolithic building has been very well articulated, inside and out, giving it both a human scale and tactile qualities.

Jangchungdan Park at the foot of Namsan has traditionally been a romantic place for the people of Seoul, and in the 1960s when the song *Foggi Jangchungdan Park* by Bae-Ho (1942–1971) was one of the most popular songs in Korea, young couples would often meet there. The park is also home to two other projects by Kim Swoo-geun: the Freedom Centre (1963) and the Tower Hotel (1969). These buildings, despite representing a previous generation, have survived the test of time. Their beautifully articulated Brutalist forms, showing the influence of Le Corbusier (1887–1965) and Kenzō Tange (1913–2005), sit harmoniously with their surroundings.

opposite Kyungdong Presbyterian Church, with stairs leading to the hidden entrance at the back.

overleaf The Space Group Building with later glass addition. It now houses the Arario Museum with restaurant.

Directly opposite, the National Theatre (1973) by Lee Hee-tae welcomes the public via a large open square, a covered walkway and a Brutalist concrete exterior with expressed, elevated columns. At the time it was built, there was an ongoing debate around ethnicity, modernization, development and tradition. Culture naturally occurs when people meet to share joy and sadness, so it was felt that a new theatre was needed in the centre of the city. Humans long for some type of landmark to mark where they live, symbolizing their emotions, values, cultural traditions and memorable events.

In western societies, monuments highlight the identity of a city and represent the collective lives of its citizens. In Korea, however, such buildings were primarily used to strengthen the authority of the ruling class, rather than for the benefit of the general public. Residents tended to meet and hold events in places where people would naturally gather, such as markets. The National Theatre is one of the interesting projects of that period, channelling social behaviour and influenced stylistically by Modernist movements, while at the same time reminiscent of traditional buildings like the Gyeonghoeru Pavilion, which Lee Hee-tae admired.

The architect of the following generation was Seung H-Sang, who both worked for and was influenced by Kim Swoo-geun and adopted his unique approach. For me, his most impactful

opposite The National Theatre, with concrete elements that take inspiration from both traditional Korean design and Modernist influences.

해오름극장

The Welcomm City office building, with the upper volume divided into four Corten-steel clad masses, which respond to the site context and create an 'urban void'.

project is Welcomm City (2000), which sits to the south of Kim's Kyungdong Presbyterian Church. Seung introduced an 'urban void', creating dynamic environments by unifying four small masses juxtaposed on a solid lower podium, with rhythmic voids in between. These smaller units can be seen as a city in themselves, with a street, park or plaza connected internally.

Complex sites like Welcomm City benefit from this dynamic interplay between volumes, as the site boundaries have to address multiple conditions. Here, the site faces onto a 30 m (98 ft)-wide street, with a typical office building on the right and lower houses sprawling to the left and rear. The architect sought solutions to questions about spatial hierarchy and the composition of central and auxiliary spaces, as well as order. Generally speaking, western architecture tends to be more centralized and less porous or permeable than the architecture of Asia. For me, Korean architecture is more improvisational and spontaneous.

GYEONGBOKGUNG PALACE

I have fond memories of the area in and around Gyeongbokgung Palace. It is most beautiful in the springtime, but still delightful in summer. The area was relatively quiet in the 1990s when I was at school. Days off were few and far between, so most people did not have time to visit the palace. On rainy days, even the ticket office would be unmanned and the doors left wide open. I would go in with my friends, and together we would wander around in the rain. Sometimes we would even fall asleep in one of the pavilions, and the guards would come along and kick us out so they could close the gates for the night. It was a truly peaceful and beautiful experience.

I have always felt content whenever I found myself at the palace. Its appearance isn't too delicate or over-designed, its proportions are balanced and it sits harmoniously at the foot of Bukaksan. Typically, the most important feature in Korean architecture is the *madang*, the outdoor space or 'space between', which can be between buildings or between walls, and is open to the elements. Perhaps that is why my most vivid memories are of weather and the changing seasons. In my early years, I spent countless hours in the *madangs* of *hanoks*. Later, I began to explore the much bigger *masa madang* of palaces, which often have trees or ponds.

The idea of the *madang* is that it is an open space connected to the interior, which serves as an indirect source of light. Sunlight bounces off the pale sandy ground and sweeps beneath the large overhang of the roof, which itself serves as protection from the downpour of seasonal monsoons. The light is diffused through doors and shutters made from handmade paper, pasted across the delicate wooden frames. When struck by light, the paper appears suffused with warm light. A deep connection is made, and the inhabitants are constantly made aware of the conditions of the outdoors, sensitive to the changing seasons and weather from day to day. They are protected, but also interact with and appreciate their environment.

In Korean culture, it is believed that any given parcel of land has an energy flow in the form of light, shadow, water and wind, and architecture tries to strike a balance between nature and humans, much like yin and yang. A version of that same ancient symbol takes centre stage in the South Korean flag, accompanied by triplets of bold black lines at each corner. Together, they represent all manner of universal truths.

TWIN TREES

Having been commissioned to design an office project in central Seoul, my first thought when I visited the site was that the building would be visible from the *madang* of Gyeongbokgung Palace (p. 20). The location was also just opposite Dongshipjagak Gate, formerly a guard tower for the palace. The stone base dates from the late 14th century in the early Joseon dynasty (1392–1897), and the structure on top was commissioned by Prince Daewongun in the mid-1800s.

It was paramount that the building's sharp corners should not be visible, and that its overall appearance would not be too severe within the sensitive context. The site is on a bend in a busy road, so my second thought was about the experience pedestrians and vehicles would have when coming around the corner. By designing undulating shapes, seventeen storeys high, which wrap around the street, an interesting visual effect would be created, further amplified by a monolithic yet dynamic glass façade that would appear solid from the street.

When designing this movement of volumes on site, it was important to create a connection with the fabric of the pre-existing building, including the alleys behind it, and its relationship to the palace. This was reinforced by a central pathway that runs between the towers, forming a visual corridor towards Dongshipjagak Gate and the palace. The pathway allows for pedestrian movement and an outside sitting area, and ultimately creates a dialogue between different parts of the city. For me, architecture exists in the 'in-between' space defined by the paradoxes of public and private, urban and natural, open and bound. It is between these paradoxes that a holistic unity of the building is achieved, a single entity in relation to humans and the natural world, which acts as a passageway crossing all boundaries.

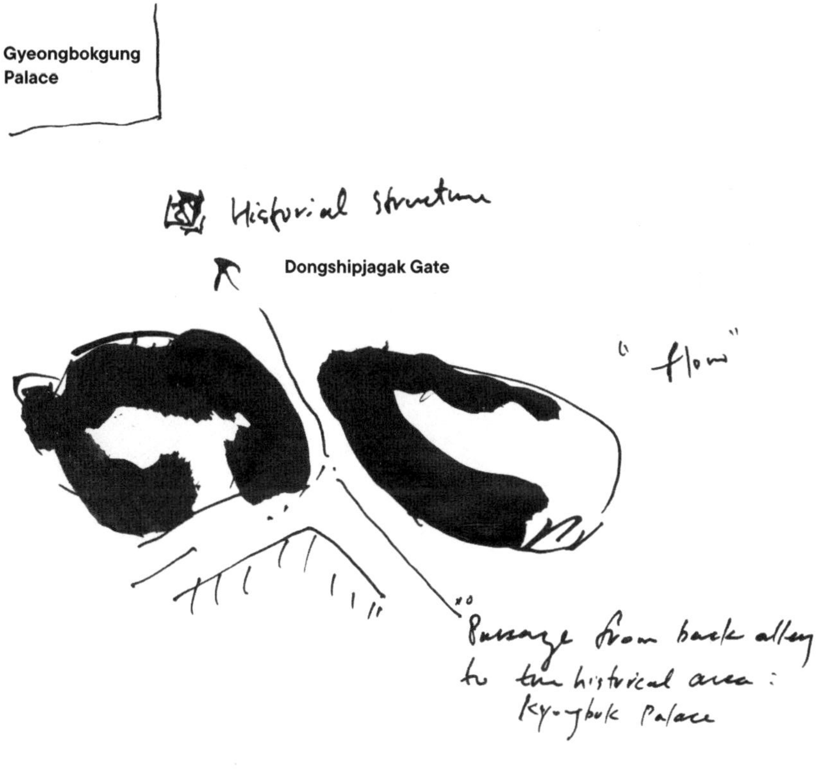

Gyeongbokgung
Palace

Historical structure

Dongshipjagak Gate

"flow"

Passage from back alley
to the historical area:
Kyongbuk Palace

Looking from Gyeongbokgung Palace towards Twin Trees, with its undulating façade smoothing out the corners of the towers.

BUKCHON

Bukchon is probably where the 600-year-old historic fabric of Seoul is best preserved. It sits harmoniously on a hill between Gyeongbokgung Palace (p. 20) and the early 15th-century Changdeok Palace, from which Biwon Secret Garden (1395) can be easily reached on foot. Here, flowers, trees, shrubs and herbs have been left to grow and blossom without the intervention of human hands, except when necessary. Several pavilions, lotus ponds, fountains and landscaped lawns sprawl across the soft hills, along with an astonishing number of different plant species, with some trees over 300 years old.

To the south of Changdeok Palace is Jongmyo Royal Shrine, built in 1394 and rebuilt in 1608. According to UNESCO it is the oldest Confucian royal shrine to have been preserved, and it is one of my favourite places in Korea. The 150 m (492 ft)-long linear wooden structure sits on a podium above a series of irregular stones that form a straight line. The stones represent the path followed by the emperor's soul when it leaves the world. The emphasis is on elongated horizontal lines, with a roughly cut stone base and sharp wooden details. The shrine has two ceremonial halls, and houses ancestral tablets of the emperors and their families. A series of sculptures protects it from bad spirits.

The space does not draw attention to itself, but radiates a monumental stillness, echoing the meditative rituals that are carried out inside. Apart from the raised podium with its rough-cut stones, my favourite feature of the shrine is the *dancheong*, or composition of opposing colours, particularly the use of green on the surfaces of the wooden elements against the purple-red of the main public structures. As well as the podium's rough stones, the use of colour seems to be a continuation of the idea of restraint, reflecting Confucius's belief in minimum intervention with any natural phenomenon, leaving colours, shapes and textures in their most honest state.

Narrow alleyways lined with small adjacent *hanoks* radiate off Bukchon-ro, the main street, which was a narrow lane until about twenty-five years ago. The houses that faced onto it had delicate, beautiful façades. Even though the street has lost some of that original refinement, its alleys are very much in their original condition, and there are interesting buildings dedicated to art – including the Kukje Gallery (2012), the National Museum of Modern and Contemporary Art (2013) and the Songwon Art Centre (2012) – to be discovered.

The South Korean government had been based near Changdeok Palace since 1948, and the area was not popular during the period of political tension lasting until 1987. I remember people walking by and being asked for their ID. In 2022, the presidential office was moved from Bukchon. It had previously been based in the Blue House, so-called because of its blue roof tiles, which sits at the foot of Bukaksan behind the palace. The feeling was that the building represented old political beliefs that were no longer relevant.

Towards the south of Bukchon, the area becomes more institutional and the buildings larger. Jongno Tower (1999) and Seoul New City Hall (2013), also located here, break away stylistically from the traditional designs of the smaller buildings further north. Today, the area has benefited from efforts to create somewhere for creatives to meet and collaborate. It has become a neighbourhood of novelists, poets, painters, designers, film directors, artists, dancers, musicians and calligraphers. These small businesses taking pride in their craft merge with a generation of people who meet in cafés, restaurants, galleries and cosy bookstores and vinyl shops, and make the area feel intimate, communal and almost like a village again.

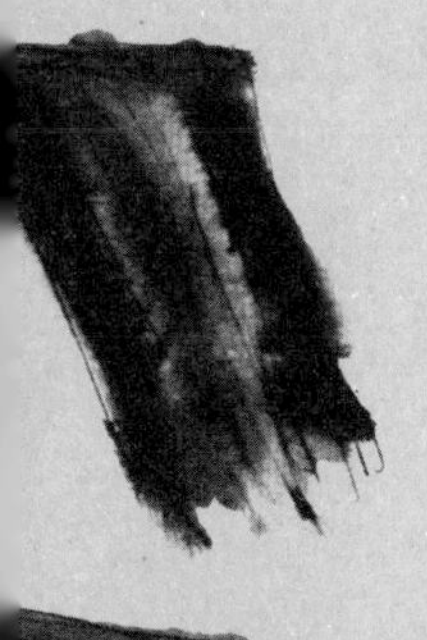
Seoul Bienalle 2023
2022

YEOL GALLERY

When I was invited to design a new office building and visited the client in their existing *hanok* office, I noticed the building next door, which had been built without much care or interesting features. I like plain buildings. They tend to reflect more honestly the time in which they were built – in this case, the penurious 1970s. As the client was a non-profit organization for traditional arts and crafts, I suggested that they buy this plain, humble building and fix it up. I stressed the importance of keeping alive some values that might not seem attractive at first, but that perform an important service by representing a particular period of time truthfully and sincerely. The client accepted my suggestion, and gave up the idea of building a completely new structure on a separate site.

The building mass was kept as it was, with windows and doors replaced and relocated with some façade changes. Most of the existing structural components and the external envelope were preserved. Owing to the weak structure and weathering, however, along with the aging materials, additional reinforcement and repair were needed. Since the original interior layout was not suitable for exhibitions, a new large space was created by exposing the load-bearing concrete walls and beams, forming a double-height space in the basement with natural lighting. Plywood boxes were placed on top of the existing beams on ground level to create additional exhibition space with controlled lighting and a warm atmosphere. The boxes provide a more easily organized area for display, and the gap between them provides space for a downstairs loo.

The new façade focuses on exposing the existing brick by placing large glass panels, hung on metal clips, at a respectful distance in front. This achieves an ordered visual appearance from the street, with large windows opening up the building, on the one hand; on the other, it offers opportunities to be reminded of the history of the original building.

Plywood boxes for exhibition spaces sit lightly on top of existing concrete beams left from the partial demolition of the floor.

4TH SEOUL BIENNALE OF ARCHITECTURE AND URBANISM

The neighbourhood of Songhyeon-dong, meaning 'pine tree hill', was a buffer zone southeast of Gyeongbokgung Palace (p. 20). After 100 years of occupation by the Japanese and then the Americans, who used it for housing US embassy employees, the site finally opened to the public in October 2022. The city of Seoul plans to use it eventually as a park with a museum, but until construction begins, the site has been made available for public events.

As the general director of the 4th Seoul Biennale of Architecture and Urbanism 2023 with the theme 'Land Architecture, Land Urbanism', I took inspiration from the site's history and its astonishing view towards the mountains in the north. These mountains define the edge of Seoul, and were instrumental parameters when the city was laid out in 1393 along the principles of divination based on topography. The location, therefore, is significant in terms of its identity.

The two main pavilions built for the Biennale are Tangso ('earth place') and Haneulso ('heaven/sky place'), and the design for both stemmed from the strong relationship of the site to its surroundings. One of the pavilions is set below ground in order to best appreciate the open landscape and view of the mountains, and the other is above ground to direct visitors' gaze towards the axis of the city.

All of the structural components and construction materials will be 100 per cent recycled, including earth, water, gravel and scaffolding. The scaffolding will be carefully dismantled after the event has ended and used for another function. In this way, the architecture is not only integrated into nature visually, but also structurally, creating a holistic assimilation that is suitable for somewhere as special as Songhyeon-dong.

opposite, above Tangso, with Bukaksan and Bukhansan visible beyond. The pond reflects the sky and the surrounding landscape.

opposite, below Haneulso, with viewing platform and fabric installation for experiencing wind and light, and views of the sky.

SEOCHON AND YEONHUI-DONG

Like Bukchon, Seochon ('west village') is one of the oldest neighbourhoods in Seoul. The name refers to its location west of Gyeongbokgung Palace (p. 20) at the foot of Inwangsan (Bukchon is east of the palace). Easily accessible from Gyeongbokgung Station, Seochon is characterized by its many *hanoks*, narrow alleyways and modern galleries, as well as Tongin Market, which dates back to 1941 when Korea was still under Japanese rule, and now comprises around seventy stalls and restaurants. This cohesion of *hanoks*, Japanese-style architecture, galleries and outdoor markets is truly unique.

Until 1945, Japanese officials working for the governor lived in Seochon, which is why some houses have Japanese-style roofs. Following the liberation of Korea, artists and craftspeople settled here, turning the area into an artistic village with many galleries. Today, the best way to discover it is by wandering along its many alleyways with no particular destination in mind. Among the details that reference the past are old carvings on stones and fences made from roof tiles.

Over the last ten years, the neighbourhood has been transformed with the arrival of galleries, cafés, boutiques and bookshops. I discovered the area because I liked visiting a particular bookshop. Others who come here may also be looking for a more mindful, offline and comfortable context within these old buildings and streets, which for so long quietly co-existed while urbanization took hold in other parts of the city.

An alley in Seochon, where one can hear people chatting and cooking inside their houses. Warm light filters through the windows and shadows are cast on the stone paving.

The Art Museum of Park No-Su is an interesting place in which to travel back in time. Formerly the home of the artist Park No-su (1973–2011), the building dates to 1937 and was designed by Park Gil-ryong, who combined western and Japanese architecture. Today, the house has been transformed into a small museum, with the artist's works displayed in the living room and bedroom, and views of the surrounding hills from the creaking wooden stairs.

Along with older buildings, there are also successful contemporary additions that reflect the complex cultural fabric of this part of the city. Next to the palace is the Arumjigi Building (2013), designed by Kim Jongkyu. I was a member of the building committee, and remember looking at the proposals for the site. I was intrigued by the simple elegance of Kim's design, and felt that it would sit nicely in this context. The façade has a lower section in exposed concrete, a timber-clad middle section and a translucent glass top that blurs into the sky. Inside, it reflects elements of traditional Korean design, with movable partitions and a replica of a *hanok* on the ground floor, where activities can take place around the *madang*. *Arumjigi* means 'people who preserve and take care of our beautiful culture', and the building pays tribute to that idea.

Another interesting building further north on the same street is Onjium (2018), an adaptive reuse of an existing building by One O One Architects, which contains a restaurant that serves traditional royal Korean cuisine. From the outside, it looks calm, with a clear distinction between solid and void elements. The lobby space integrates timber elements of the Goryeo dynasty (918–1392), linking back to the appearance of the nearby palace. Transparent partitions and reflective surfaces guide visitors while creating a flow of spaces that extend into the canopies of the trees flanking the street.

Since Bukchon and Seochon are two of the only neighbourhoods that still have *hanoks*, the government contributes money to their preservation and upkeep. Unfortunately, structures that are not classified as *hanoks* are demolished and replaced with new, more profitable building types. What gets lost is the cultural value of the street. I believe it is the architect's role to unravel the layers of history, build upon what is already there and preserve the sense of identity that has been established in a particular area over the years.

GIZI Exhibition and Residence (p. 48), my project for the artist Park Seo-bo, focuses on capturing Korean identity. The building is set a little further west of Seochon in Yeonhui-dong, near Ansan mountain. More new large buildings dominate the streets here than in Seochon, but as it is set in the foothills of the mountain, the essence of the space remains similar.

PROJECT SPACE MAHK

Project Space Mahk – which we call 'Mahk-jip' – involved the renovation of an old *hanok* so that it could be used for exhibitions, installations and forums. It is the embodiment of my personal architectural philosophy, which takes inspiration from the Korean idea of *bium* and *mahk*, or sense of emptiness and simplicity.

I have also grown up with the influence of my father, who said 'to go beyond is as wrong as to be short'. There is a beauty in humility that takes us back to nature and the straightforward relationship between the elements. In my architectural designs, the way that light and air move through a building, as well as its harmonious relationship to the ground and its context, are key considerations. Perhaps this attitude, which is characteristic of Korean culture, derives from the limitations of living within extreme climate conditions and is affected by socio-political factors.

In the past, Korea was influenced by foreign cultures, including those of China, Japan and western countries, but has not been defined by their distinct idiosyncrasies. For example, the Japanese courtyard is about observation and the Chinese courtyard is about organized hierarchy, but the Korean courtyard is about emptiness. This space might be used for eating, playing or making music, but in its essence, the emptiness remains for contemplation. Korean architecture is less ostentatious, more self-sufficient and meditative. Another example is the Japanese idea of *wabi-sabi*, which describes a humble experience that is similar to the Korean concept of *mahk*. This places the process of making at its heart, so that the result is not about creating a certain impression. Instead of trying to make an object that looks humble, in other words, the appearance is an after-effect that cannot be controlled.

opposite For this project, a *hanok* from 1910 was refurbished, with the original structure and finishes left exposed. A moon jar can be seen in the window.

Exterior view of Mahk-jip, looking into the exhibition space from the street.

The term *mahk* suggests something that is overlooked, or lacking in finesse. *Makgeolli*, for instance, is a popular Korean alcoholic beverage made from steamed rice, yeast and water left to ferment in a clay pot, while Seungmu dance is characterized by leaving space for improvisation, making each performance unique. *Mahk* is a rejection of refinement for the sake of refinement. It is matter of fact, but also recognizes that space should be reserved for some elusive higher power. *Bium* might be translated as 'emptiness', and draws on the belief of the Confucian *sunbi*, or the connection between universal pathos and the act of creating. Instead of focusing solely on dogmatic principles, it celebrates the process of making. Metaphorically speaking, this process can be compared to making pottery. One piece of pottery will never be exactly the same as another, and is therefore authentic in telling a story about the way it was made.

Lee Ufan, an influential Korean painter and theorist, identifies the moon jar as the epitome of these aesthetic principles. Moon jars (see p. 39), a type of Korean white porcelain, originated in the Joseon dynasty (1392–1897), and are made by joining two hemispherical bowls to form one large spherical shape. It is impossible to make a jar in one piece, as its large size means that the clay would not be able to support itself during the drying process. The jar's true appeal comes from this process and reflects, as Lee Ufan says, a 'lack of completeness and presence as an artwork'. Contemporary ceramicists like Young Sook Park and Dong Jun Kim still work with moon jars and interpret them in their own ways.

Mahk-jip, a space created inside a traditional *hanok*, represents the essence of *bium* and *mahk*. The existing condition of the *hanok* was preserved by celebrating its unfinished surfaces and efficient use of space and material. No clear symmetry governs the space, and the rooms of varied sizes flow into one another. Visitors can move freely through the interior and exterior spaces. Architecture is a phenomenon that has an organic relationship with people's memories and emotions from the past, and expectations for what will take place in the future.

ONGROUND CAFÉ GALLERY

Across the street from Mahk-jip (p. 38) is the Onground Café Gallery, a renovation project involving two adjoining buildings: a 100-year-old Japanese house and a 1960s commercial building. This is another adaptive reuse project that experiments with the properties of *mahk* by adapting a space to provide a new experience and reveal time and memory. It now hosts a café and gallery as a place for communication and dialogue.

'Onground' implies standing on two feet with a strong, confident stance. I designed the space to speak boldly about its identity. Removing the walls and roof tiles uncovered the hidden wooden structure and reintroduced the attractive effect of sunlight filtering through the cracks of the wooden boards. It also revealed the beauty and simplicity present in the old skeleton of the house, although it was to become an exhibition space with limited light. The existing posts and beams were kept intact, and glass was placed on top.

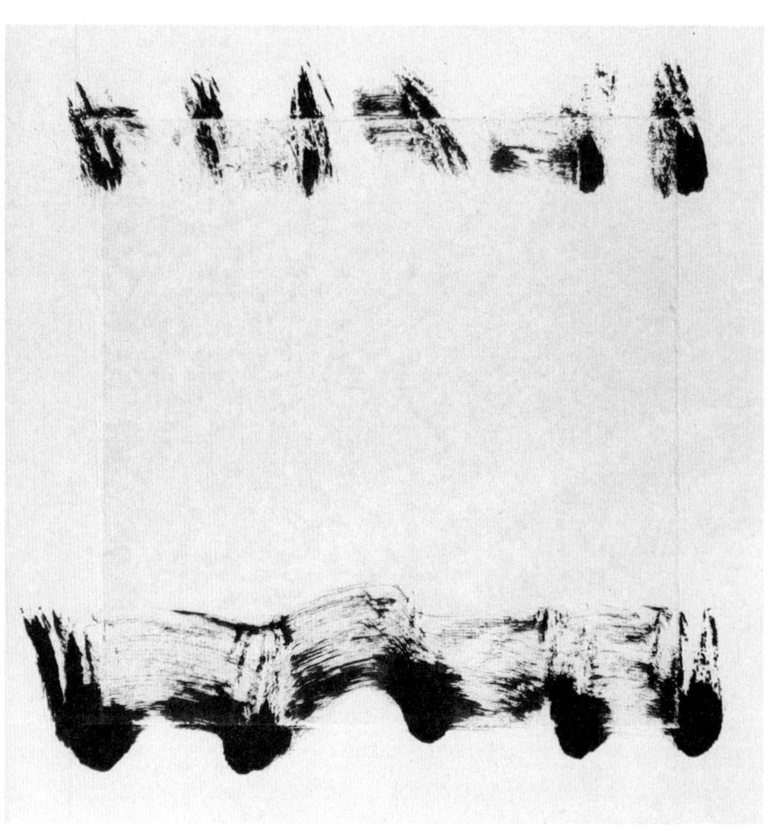

opposite In my art studio in Seochon, in *mahk*-painting action.
above One of my works, *Mahk* (2022), in black ink on Korean paper.

overleaf The café, with its original wooden structure. The roof tiles were replaced with glass, allowing light to flood into the space.

The project set out to create a new space by combining existing values with new ideas.

White-rendered walls provide a contrast to the dark wooden finish, while creating a screen for the shadows cast through the building. Some of the walls and partitions were cut through to reveal their inner layers and acquire a new continuum of spaces. Upon entering, visitors to the café are guided through multiple open rooms and a small courtyard towards the back, which takes inspiration from the principles of a *hanok*. Small trees were also planted to express the beauty and comfort that comes from the little things in everyday life.

Onground Café Gallery is a reflection on architecture and its impact on the social context by recognizing that human behaviour is empirical. The building, therefore, influences an individual's communication with a bound place, changing how we move through it, our state of mind, how we perceive the people around us and our perception of its history.

Rather than sharp tools, a bamboo stick with rounded corners is typically used to form the edges of the *mahksabal*.

THEGROUND MUSIC AND ART STUDIO

Located on an infill site north of the Onground Café Gallery (p. 42), Theground has a café space, a music bar in the basement and my art studio upstairs. I am passionate about art and music, and this project is very special to me. The strict setbacks stipulated by building regulations led to its irregular shape, and the structural lines expressed on the soffit internally mimic the seemingly unordered directions of the beams. In the basement, a glazed segment of the ground-floor slab visually connects the music bar with the café space above.

From the outside, the windows are large and theatrical, their forms and dimensions imitating the openings of the traditional urban fabric and displaying a sense of playfulness across the otherwise monolithic façade. From inside, they allow extensive views over the *hanok* roofs of Seochon towards Inwangsan. Large, sliding wooden shutters placed in front of the windows regulate the intensity of the sun and amount of privacy, and recall the movable partitions of the *hanoks*.

The way the light falls into my atelier, especially in the early morning, fills me with joy. Here, I can paint and further explore the state of *mahk*. I place a thick brush loaded with ink or oil paint, turn and push it with varying degrees of pressure, before finally releasing it, leaving traces of this energy forever captured on a piece of paper (ill. pp. 42, 43). The process is like a potter leaving behind finger marks on a *mahksabal* (a Korean rice bowl), paying tribute to the perfection inherent in the messiness of nature. The *mahksabal* is a profoundly simple form, created with utility in mind. It is made from humble, unrefined materials, and in such haste that the speed of work is visible. It has probably been the most influential object on my aesthetic values in my life, and the object that I believe most represents Korean culture.

GIZI EXHIBITION AND RESIDENCE

The GIZI Exhibition and Residence combines a studio with a reception and exhibition space, along with three residences for the artist Park Seo-bo, his son's family and his grandson. All of these functions are held together by a screen of perforated metal, which visually governs the design of the building.

Park Seo-bo's monochromatic paintings explore ideas of repetition and layering, and are rooted in the tradition of calligraphy as practised by classical scholars and monks who chant the Buddhist mantra over and over again. This method of repetition, he says, is about emptying oneself and achieving a state of dignity. It is also less about self-expression or the demonstration of one's own talent, and more about the meditative process. In my own work, this essence of emptiness is a pivotal aspect, so working with Park on this project has been rewarding in many ways.

The holes in the perforated powder-coated aluminium façade vary in size and density to create different levels of openness. This allows views to the outside, as well as privacy from other buildings and passers-by. With changing light conditions during the day, this secondary skin becomes a layer that opens and closes, casts shadows and lets in diffused sunlight. It catches the light at various angles, depending on the position of the folded metal in relation to the sun. Outside, a long, sheltered moss-covered garden connects with the interior exhibition spaces. Movable partitions sitting perpendicular to the garden serve as display space for Park's work. Visitors to the exhibition space can enjoy the connection to the outside via the sliding glass doors, which can be fully opened to make the space feel airy and spacious.

opposite, above View of the perforated metal screen, with the varying ratios of open to solid creating different degrees of permeability.

opposite, below View into the exhibition and reception area, with sliding doors that open onto the moss-covered rock garden.

PYEONGCHANG-DONG

Pyeongchang-dong is nestled in a valley formed by a section of Bukhansan that leads to Bukaksan and Inwangsan at the northern end of Jongno-gu district. Owing to its topography, Pyeongchang-dong feels like a suburb of Seoul, hidden behind mountains, valleys and greenery. Mountain ranges in South Korea tend to be smaller than, for example, the Swiss Alps or the Rockies, with the tallest being Hallasan at 1,950 m (6,398 ft).

Two-thirds of South Korea is covered by mountains, and Seoul is enclosed by them, with Bukhansan to the north, Yongmasan to the east, Gwanaksan to the south and Deokyangsan to the west. In this landscape, it becomes clear why Confucianism, Taoism and Zen Buddhism were all embraced, as they each strive for harmony with nature. On weekends, city dwellers don their hiking gear and head to the mountains to climb to the summits and enjoy *makgeolli* (rice wine) and *jeon* (Korean pancakes) afterwards. They greet each other on the way up, chat when they have a rest and enjoy the views.

Unlike other neighbourhoods in Seoul, Pyeongchang-dong is very quiet, with 65 per cent of the total area protected from development. It is an attractive residential neighbourhood with museums and galleries, hiking trails, waterways and little passages. I have completed several homes and art studios here, including '–' Shaped Studio Residence and Gugidong House, which has an open roof terrace to increase natural light, ventilation and views. I also decided to build my own home here in 2007: Four Box House, which has four overlapping boxes arranged around a central courtyard, and low horizontal windows with views out to the beautiful topography of the foothills. It has truly been a place filled with joy and a respite from the busy life of Seoul. I enjoy drinking tea with my wife Eunsil and listening to music with friends.

Nearby is Changamjang Residence (1974), by Kim Swoo-geun. From the outside, it looks like a strong, vertical, articulated brick building, but the overall concept goes far beyond that. Taking inspiration from Frank Lloyd Wright's Fallingwater (1964) in Pennsylvania, Kim placed the house harmoniously on a rock in a stream, in constant interplay with the landscape. The initial aim was to position two volumes parallel to one another, but owing to the condition of the site, they were turned at oblique angles. Large windows further amplify the connection to the landscape, and corner windows, which were quite unusual at the time, were also added. Circulation is facilitated by visual links between the spaces, as there are barely any walls and the rooms open up to double-height spaces with mezzanines.

Ten years after the completion of Changamjang Residence, the Total Museum (1984; ill. pp. 53, 54) was built. It is Korea's first privately owned contemporary art institution and was designed by Shin-Kyu Moon in partnership with the museum director Joon-Eui Noh. Shin-Kyu Moon was a key influence for me. When I returned from studying and working abroad, he was one of the pioneers when it came to using local materials in an almost impulsive manner. This had a profound effect on me as a young architect, and we developed a friendly mentor-student relationship. We still stay in contact, and I try to contribute to the countless non-profit events the museum organizes to support young artists by donating my own art and giving annual lectures.

Next door is Gana Art Centre (1998), designed by Wilmotte & Associés in collaboration with Total Design, and dedicated to contemporary art with references to Korea's artistic past. The arrangement of the interior is very successful, as it separates the public space – with its open-air theatre in the middle – from a more private space with tiered seating, reached via an aerial footbridge. Outside, monolithic blocks of white Italian stone create an area where shadows are cast, and the overall appearance is informed by large blocks lifted off the ground with passageways leading inside. Above all, the centre has established itself as a major facilitator for the local art scene. Among other activities, it organizes open-house programmes that allow people to visit the homes of painters, sculptors and other artists to gain insights into their lives and work. The director, Ho Jae Lee, also organizes a cultural forum and activities for the artists' communities. Some of my own paintings have been exhibited there.

Following the road further east leads to the Kim Chong Yung Museum (2002), dedicated to the sculptor of the same name (1915–1982). The museum, designed by Poetry Architecture, was completed in 2002; an addition was added eight years later. The two-storey building, set lower at the rear with a small stream to the east, fits well into the streetscape. The exhibition space was designed in accordance with the site topography, with the art displayed on terraced spaces that flow with the slope of the site from the highest point at

View of the approach to the Total Museum.

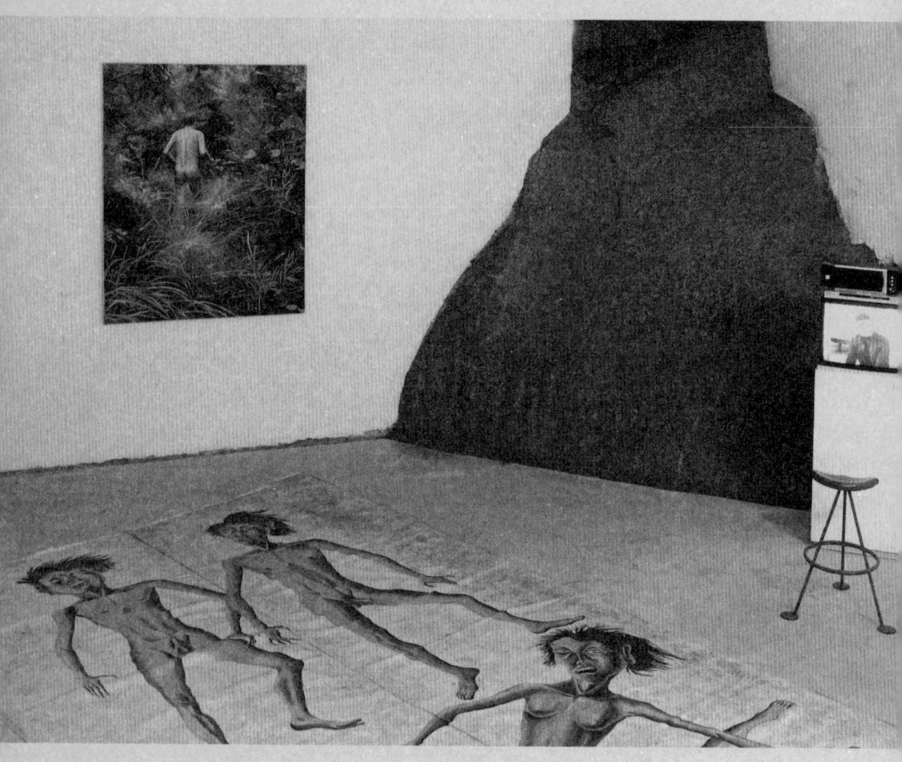

The exhibition space inside the Total Museum, which utilizes the rocks on site as a distinctive feature of the environment.

the north to the lowest point at the south. Upon entering the museum via a ramp, visitors walk into a courtyard from which they can see the overall architecture of the building, before being guided back to the courtyard after viewing the exhibition.

The museum's location next to the mountain may be why so many artists and art lovers feel inspired and at peace in this building. Koreans believe in *feng shui* and the energy of the land (*ki*), and the energy here is believed to be high owing to the presence of the mountain. Apart from the natural beauty of the landscape, there is a sense of community in Pyeongchang-dong, and it has become very precious to me.

BUAM-DONG

I pass through Buam-dong every day on my commute between my home in Pyeongchang-dong and Mahk-jip (p. 38) and my art studio in Seochon (p. 47). One of my dear projects, Buam House (ill. p. 7), is located here. It incorporates a *hanok* sitting on a hill among ancient trees with twisting trunks and branches that resemble dancers frozen in their dynamic positions.

Buam-dong is at the edge of the green belt just outside the city centre, next to Inwangsan, where the great Fortress Wall crawls up the hill. It was built during the Joseon dynasty (1392–1897) and people enjoy hiking along it. From here, set in the foothills of the mountains, the topography of Seoul can be seen. The royal families owned summer pavilions in the area, and the site of Buam House was owned by Prince Anpyeong (also known as Sejo of Joseon), the son of Sejong of Joseon (1397–1455). In his painting *Suseongdong*, the artist Jeong Seon (1676–1759) painted Buam-dong, showing the rock formation of the valley and what appears to be Giringyo Bridge in the foreground. Another of his well-known works is *Inwangjesaekdo* (*After Rain at Mt Inwang*), which also depicts the area and is designated as a National Treasure.

Being set in a historic site, the design of the *hanok* and garden at Buam House unites tradition and modernity. The garden follows the organic shapes of the topography and vegetation, with clean-cut stones guiding the way up the hill. The timber of the *hanok* and the meticulously aligned *hanji* paper on the walls and floors meet stainless-steel countertops. The small house uses *ondol*, the traditional underfloor heating system, but also has concealed electric lighting to create indirect ambient light when it gets dark. Another former royal summer residence in the area is Seokpajeong, behind the Seokpajeong Seoul Art Museum. Upon entering, visitors can access the majestic *hanok* at the back of the site. After visiting the museum, visitors can continue along Jahamun-ro 38 to the Whanki Museum, a beautiful space that displays the collection of abstract art and personal effects of the artist Whanki Kim (1913–1974).

Further south is the Yoon Dong-ju Literature Museum. One of my projects, Earth House (p. 104), is dedicated to the poet Yoon Dong-ju (1917–1945) and his collection of poems about the sky, wind and stars. I find him truly fascinating, and I enjoy reading his poems, which he wrote while imprisoned during the Korean independence movement. Nearby is the Changuimun Gate (1396), which marks the starting point of one of many hiking trails in the area and is the most northwesterly of the 'Eight Gates of Seoul'.

When I find myself in Buam-dong – and I do spend a lot of time here – I find it remarkable how close it is to downtown Seoul, and how it still feels intrinsically different owing to its quiet atmosphere and connection with the natural world.

overleaf Stone steps lead up to Buam House's *hanok* on the hill. Granite steps pass by a 400-year-old zelkova tree on the right and an ancient boulder covered in moss brought from Mungyeong in Gyeongsang province.

HANNAM-DONG

Hannam-dong is in Yongsan-gu, near the centre of Seoul. It owes its name to its location between the Han River and Namsan mountain. Centuries ago, it was simply a rural area on the outskirts of the city, but in the second half of the 19th century the rapid developments that transformed Seoul into a sprawling concrete metropolis with improved traffic systems also connected Gangbuk in the north with Gangnam in the south.

Today, Hannam-dong is a popular area to live for locals and foreigners. The American embassy and the United States Forces Korea unit were located nearby, making it easy to access emerging cultures. Many Koreans who had moved abroad for education returned to establish new businesses here, influenced by foreign culture mixed with K-Style. When wandering around the streets, the vivacious mix of bars, coffee shops, fashion stores and international restaurants is clearly evident.

Like Seongsu-dong (p. 64) to the east, Hannam-dong and the neighbouring Itaewon became very popular. But while Seongsu-dong is characterized by large warehouses sitting on flat land, Hannam-dong and Itaewon are both set within the foothills of Namsan and have many narrow alleyways. The view towards Namsan is protected, and buildings are limited to a few storeys in height. Most houses have flat roofs that are used as roof terraces with panoramic views over the urban sprawl, with each house displaying a refined and captivating sense of asymmetry. Namsan and Namsan Tower together form the backdrop to the scene.

Leading east to west, Itaewon-ro (the main road) loosely separates the more residential area in the north from the bustling leisure centre to the south. The northern section has a steep incline towards Namsan, where my design for the E-Shaped House tenderly embraces the landscape by opening up the building mass to welcome in the garden, as well as a water feature with views to the south.

To the east is the Leeum Samsung Museum of Art, comprising three different buildings, each designed by a different architect: Mario Botta, Jean Nouvel and Rem Koolhaas. There are also many smaller galleries, including Thaddaeus Ropac and the Pace Gallery, near Hangangjin Station and designed by Mass Studies. Branching off Itaewon-ro is Daesagwan-ro, where another of my projects is located: Hannam-dong Office (p. 62). There are many interesting buildings in the area, and I often visit them. Music gives me a lot of joy, and I have a passion for collecting old vinyl and speaker systems. The Hyundai Card Music Library designed by Choi Moongyu is an interesting space for finding rare vinyl.

HANNAM-DONG OFFICE

The context of the site for this project was complex, with small buildings dotted about without any unity. The building, therefore, had to have a strong identity in its function as an office. The south façade is the main elevation, and six rectangular openings of varying sizes were cut into the concrete wall enveloping the underlying mass. The wall is structural, but offset from the building. In its urban context, it becomes a buffer from the complexity of the surrounding neighbourhood. Large openings in the north and south façades provide ventilation; to the east and west, more concrete structural walls support the post-tension slabs to create column-free interior spaces and hide the nearby buildings from view.

Inside, the finishes focus on wooden surfaces with warm red cedar siding inside the exposed concrete outer wall. The plywood on the ceiling resolves sound absorption and lighting, and gives the space warmth. Balconies at the north of the building have bamboo forests to introduce a sense of connection to nature in this otherwise urban setting. The design store and landscaped entry area provide a friendly human-scale experience for pedestrians approaching the building from the main road.

The project aims to create a private space in the city. Further down the street is another project with the same kind of focus that I like. Sounds Hannam contains multiple activities that would be typically found in a city within a single building. The name refers back to the notion of a multitude of voices creating a sound, implying that in urban areas many different activities happen simultaneously, often in a hectic manner. It is important for an individual to stay focused and find their own rhythm in order to co-exist in a healthy way within this bigger system.

The double-layered concrete wall works as a buffer between the interior space and the busy street.

성
수
동

SEONGSU-DONG

Located in the southwest portion of the city and bordered by the Han River and the Jungnangcheon Stream, Seongsu-dong is a former industrial area that is today characterized by the Seoul Forest Park and factory adaptive reuse projects. The Lotte World Tower is also nearby.

Historically, the main industrial areas of Seoul have been Guro-gu and Seongsu-dong. With the urban expansion of the city, however, those areas became residential in the 1990s. Seongsu-dong is often described as the 'Brooklyn of Seoul', with Gangnam across the river as Manhattan. At the beginning of this urban shift, the vast empty shells of the old factories lured small businesses to Seongsu-dong as they were easy to adapt. Larger companies soon followed, tempted by the opportunities for more space. Seongsu-dong does not have many historical landmarks, and building regulations tend to be less strict. The urban plan also allows for a higher density in this area, offering lucrative scope for development.

Today, the business district of Seongsu-dong is occupied mainly by IT companies and has evolved into a popular destination, with cafés, restaurants and fashion stores. ECS (Eatery Culture Seongsu; p. 68), a venue with multiple restaurants on various levels, and an interior-design project for the fashion and fabric company W Mission (2023) are my first projects in Seongsu-dong, and I am excited to see how the neighbourhood will develop in the future. Already a number of interesting projects have been built that deal with questions of adaptive reuse and how to design in an area with a higher floor space to land ratio.

Seongsu WAVE Commercial Building (2022) and Patema Inverted (2020) are just two such projects completed in recent years.

Daelim Warehouse on Seongsui-ro is a lively café, art gallery and event venue in an industrial red-brick building where local artists can display their work. High ceilings with exposed steel trusses define the space; light fittings or works of art can also be suspended from these trusses, making the space highly adaptive. Rustic-looking walls and salvaged metal doors add to the industrial spirit. I think this type of furniture, doors and lamps are beautiful. It reminds me of the concept of *mahk*, as the various items were designed and manufactured with function in mind. These objects do not pretend to be something that they are not. They are honest.

Another notable space is Café Onion Seongsu. Formerly a metal factory in the 1970s, it is now a popular café. From the outside, it is possible to get a sense of the test of time the building has had to withstand, and how little care has been taken to maintain it. The building never had to impress or look polished in any way, only to work. Openings were added crudely, windows of varying sizes and positions defined the elevations, and balustrades, cables and pipes were fixed without any attempt at design. Yet there is a sense of melancholy, as well as community, when visitors wander through the spaces. Perhaps one becomes more aware of the passage of time and how everything is somehow connected. The café offers different areas for enjoying coffee and food, ranging from a roof terrace on the upper level to small courtyards and a number of semi-enclosed rooms with broad communal tables.

One response to the question of how to integrate larger buildings successfully into the urban fabric is an office project called Wooran Foundation (2018) by System Lab, not far from Café Onion and Daelim Warehouse. The building offers an area of about 15,000 m^2 (161,459 sq ft) and also houses the architect's office on the sixth floor. The volume is divided into small segments to absorb its context. From the outside, it appears fragmented, almost pixel-like. A lower volume sitting beneath the tower took inspiration from the iconic shape of the pitched roofs of the factory buildings surrounding it.

The fragmented façade offers unique views of the cityscape, and provides natural light and air circulation for the workers inside. Some terraces offer areas for relaxation and break up the space even further, responding to the human scale. Photographs were taken of the neighbourhood before deciding on the materials to be used for the building. This mapping exercise led to the use of concrete with vertical grooves to give texture and tactility. Internally, the industrial atmosphere is a prevailing theme in the form of metal fit-out elements and high ceilings.

SEONGSU-DONG

ECS (EATERY CULTURE SEONGSU)

This project was designed to house numerous eateries in one building, across multiple levels, with the focus on providing outdoor dining terraces that face onto the main street. This idea stems from the concept of the *hanok*. A *mahru* is a space within the *hanok* that serves as an intermediate area, and could be described as a type of veranda. It is lifted off the ground and open to the outside, sheltered by a large roof overhang, and is a space that is partially inside and outside. Here, people are connected to the alley or street, allowing conversation with passers-by. The space also offers a sense of protection and privacy. This balance between enclosure and openness was the inspiration for the project.

The site is located in the middle of a rapidly developing commercial area, and the building fully embraces this context by opening up to the busy street. People who visit the restaurants or are seated on the terraces can experience the flow of air and light, as well as observe the street below. Transparent vinyl curtains along the glazed façade work as a means of climate control, but also create a visual effect to spark interest in the people walking by. The image of a curtain evokes a dramatic effect, both providing a lightweight separation between spaces and suggesting that there is more to see without knowing what is hidden behind it. The fact that the dining experience is spread across multiple levels adds to the lively atmosphere, and makes the building a destination where people can gather, enjoy a meal and have conversations.

For me, excellent architecture addresses the question of how to honour the existing nature of a place, and allows ground and people to exist in dialogue with one another. It is not preoccupied with how to design a building that looks impressive and begs for attention. Instead, it responds to the inherent ecological and emotive temperament of the site, so that the architecture itself expands beyond just being an artificial construct on a piece of land.

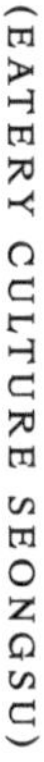

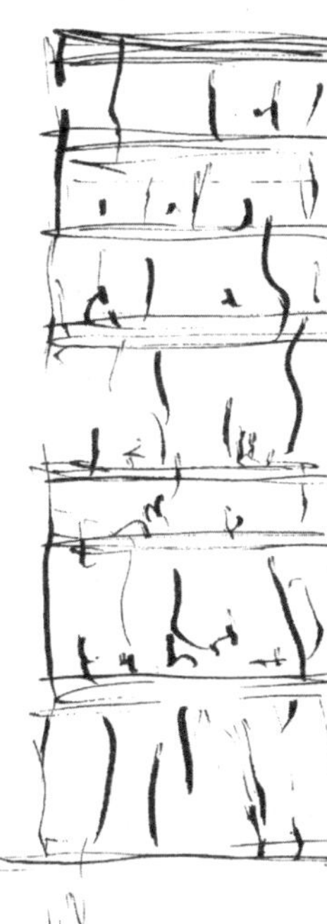

Render showing the different levels of the restaurants, with their terraces and curtains.

GANGNAM

'Gangnam' is broadly understood as the area south of the Han River. It has been subject to rapid development since the 1970s, and differs quite significantly from Gangbuk to the north. When looking at a map of Seoul, the differences between the two halves of the city become clear. In Gangnam, the streets follow a strong, orthogonal grid, whereas north of the river the streets follow a more organic path. It is important to remember that traditional Korean architecture begins with natural surroundings, such as mountains, rivers and hills, and then buildings are added, rather than implying an order first and building the space around it.

Cheongdam-dong is a ward of Gangnam district near Seongsu-dong (p. 64), which lies to the east. The name 'Cheongdam' comes from the ponds found along the south side of the Han River, surrounded by gently sloping hills, in the Joseon dynasty. During the development of Gangnam, art galleries began to move into the area, followed by fashion stores. The gentle hills have been preserved, but the smaller residential buildings have been replaced with four- or five-storey commercial buildings, a reflection of the area's growing wealth and rising property prices.

A 760 m (2,493 ft)-long section of the main street Apgujeong-ro, which runs from Apgujeongrodeo Station by the Galleria Department Store (2004) to the Cheongdam crossroads, is known as 'Cheongdam Fashion Street'. Many high-end fashion stores designed by renowned architects stand competitively, shoulder-to-shoulder. Some of the more interesting buildings are Louis Vuitton Maison (2019) by Frank Gehry, Dior Boutique (2015) by Christian de Portzamparc and Peter Marino, and the Chungha Building (2013) by MVRDV. There is no inherent architectural language; instead, each store makes a statement for itself. The backstreets and alleys behind them reveal more intriguing moments with cafés, small shops, galleries and restaurants. Comparatively, they feel more intricate and full of life.

The area has become an entertainment district, and each day it is visited by many people as it is near Seolleung Station and Starfield COEX Mall, which has been stagnant since it was remodelled in the mid-2010s. Gangnam Station is another area that gets very crowded, especially at night when people swarm the area after work to have a drink and something to eat. Upon emerging from the subway exit, visitors are greeted by flashing neon lights advertising the latest fashions or the newest beauty products, and there is a constant stream of people looking at their phones and searching for their friends. Traffic rushes past, and the smell of the fuel from the cars is pungent. The noise merges with the sound of people talking, interrupted occasionally by loud music from the many shops enticing people to enter. This irresistible vitality creates an intense buzz. Yet it is an urban space that has no history, where restaurants and shops constantly open and close in accordance with shifting tastes and trends.

In a society where life feels sped up and flooded with information, it is important to retain a sense of grounding. I believe that for architecture to have a lasting effect on someone, it is necessary to evoke a true feeling. What the

유학·연수
YBM
토익은 토익에게 물어봐!
상담·접수
7°

eye visualizes is not that important; it is what one feels at a certain moment that lasts. At the end of the day, it doesn't matter what people say to one another, but rather how someone makes another human being feel. That is why architecture must respond on a more personal level, drawing on the concepts of experience and perception.

In a dense urban environment like Gangnam, a single building can be seen as a small city sliced up into smaller segments. People lose interest if everything looks identical and design principles follow the same order. They lose attention when they cannot relate to a building. A sense of discovery and exploration must be retained, along with a straightforward simplicity, otherwise buildings become detached from the street and the result is a city that feels cold and anonymous.

Urban Hive (2008), designed by Kim In-cheurl of Archium and located near Mario Botta's Kyobo Tower (2003), is a good example of how a tall building responds well to its immediate street context. Hundreds of circular apertures, replicating the structural strength of a honeycomb, perforate the reinforced concrete wall and allow views out, as well as preserve a sense of enclosure at this busy junction. The load-bearing façade also enables the interior spaces to be largely free from supporting structures, maximizing space for its users, and creates thermal mass for efficient energy consumption, as it blocks

opposite A typical scene in Gangnam with its crowded pavement, especially in the evening and at weekends.

overleaf Triangular cut-outs in Urban Hive's concrete outer wall create an interesting entrance at ground level.

URBAN HIVE

out the sun in summer and stores heat in winter. A large triangular opening at ground level marks the entry point and creates a dialogue with the street.

Further south and built at around the same time is Boutique Monaco: Missing Matrix (2008) by Minsuk Cho of Mass Studies. It is a commercial building with cultural and community spaces on the lower levels and offices above. To maximize the amount of light, the plan is C-shaped and extruded in shifting orientation to the maximum height allowed. The fifteen 'missing' areas have inserted gardens and draw in natural light and visual links to neighbours and the natural word. By breaking the building into smaller segments, it achieves a human scale, despite its large volume. I believe it is another successful example of urban design that contributes to Gangnam, as well as providing a vivid and unique experience to the residents and tenants who live and work within its walls.

opposite Boutique Monaco: Missing Matrix by Mass Studies, with its clearly defined plinth and openings for terraces on the upper levels.

BE-TWIXT

The concept behind this project began with an ambition to conduct an experiment by applying the smaller-scale design language and grounded characteristics of alleyways to a large-scale commercial grid and structure. There is a direct connection to the street, as the alleyway protruding from the building draws people in. This alley continues and connects to the stairs and upper floors, forming a welcoming entry point.

Two shifting volumes are defined around an open central linear void with connecting bridges. Windows to each side of the linear void are placed so that they do not face each other directly, and allow natural light to bounce all the way to the bottom of the vestibule, which also provides natural ventilation into the centre

The alley splitting the two concrete masses of BE-Twixt works as a lobby space with access to the main stair and elevator.

of the building. The hallways on both sides of this central circulation space are lit by natural light, and help to orient visitors. The fourth and fifth floors have private exterior gardens and decks built on an intimate scale to provide a direct connection to air and light, forming small *madangs*. At the south of the plot, visitors can enter the recently completed ST SongEun Building (2021) by Herzog & de Meuron via a small garden.

My thesis at university was called 'Experience and Perception'. In it, I suggested that what the eye visualizes is not important, and what really matters is the experience that will be remembered. I think this idea is more common in Asian culture, whereas visual imagery is more prominent in the west. Greek temples used columns that were Doric in style, then Ionic, and then Corinthian, because it was believed that the different proportions or details were important. In Asia, however, there are not as many different styles. Rather, the emphasis was on the topography, location of a building and its relationship to nature. Greek temples are beautiful to the eye, but walking in your own neighbourhood where you feel at home is beautiful to the mind. This deep sensation of peace we feel in certain environments is what makes architecture so special.

RAMP BUILDING

The relationship between building and city can often be uninviting, resulting in banal and tense associations that are lacking in scale and sensibility. In Gangnam, with its rapid development of plots, this seems like one of the more serious issues in architecture. How do we weave new building blocks into the existing fabric of the surrounding streets and neighbourhoods?

The Ramp Building (2004) celebrates this relationship by glorifying the existing border conditions in order to entice people into exploring the site via a new passageway. Sitting on a busy street corner, it connects public and semi-public, while exploiting the naturally staggered levels from south to west. A cave-like ramp creates an unusual access into the building and provides a unique opportunity, allowing the city to move in and out of the building and offering intriguing views from a long, low window. The site is enveloped and defined by a gently curving wire screen that wraps around the corner, following the exact boundary of the site. This 'non-place' on the periphery becomes an almost symbolic gesture, allowing visitors to experience the spaces and materiality differently, inside and out.

A wine bar on the lower level was designed to be dark and primitive, with one of the few light sources being a window that overlooks a waterfall in a deep crevasse. This void creates an opportunity for exploring the boundaries of the site. The main cubic mass of the building is lifted from the chaotic ground floor and kept as pure as possible with a column-free interior. The pure abstraction is juxtaposed by punctuations using different materials and the organic ground floor, creating a transitional space. The emphasis is on how visitors encounter the in-between spaces when passing through the building, which was designed so that they experience natural air circulation and unique light movement, as well as interesting visual relationships.

Ramp Building's corridor allows neighbours to pass through the building via a concrete ramp and wire screen above.

A BY BOM

Nestled among the many buildings along Cheongdam-dong's main street is the popular hair salon A By Bom. Here, the ambition was to place a simple building that would interact with the ground in a variety of ways. It is set back as much as possible, so that it does not demand attention, with a green space connecting the building with the street. The ground floor offers one large, open space without any interruption from structural supports, such as columns.

The hair salons are on the second and fourth floors, and large windows allow clients to observe the street below, creating a visual dialogue with the action taking place. I personally enjoy looking out of a window, especially when I am watching a scene from an angle, such as an elevated or lower viewpoint, or from across the street. The relationship to what is happening becomes more interesting by being able to observe the foreground and background. In the same way a traditional Korean house is a continuum of spaces, I like how this connection can be achieved in architecture, ensuring that people are reminded of their roles in this intricate chain of events happening simultaneously all around them. When observing the goings-on in a city, the connection of a building to its context is crucial in defining the space. Having large, vertically sliding automatic windows (4.5 × 4.5 m, or 177 × 177 in.) also allows for efficient ventilation. I prefer natural ventilation and light, even when building regulations require mechanized ventilation to also be installed.

The triangular corner cut-outs at the top of the building volume provide a strong relationship to the street, especially on the sloped hill to the east, framing the view of the busy streetscape. They also introduce natural light and ventilation. The lower part of the triangle works as a skylight for the third floor, and the upper area forms part of a balcony space, offering a healthy environment for plants owing to its exposure to light and air.

above The windows slide open to allow views onto the street below.

overleaf A triangular cut-out at roof level frames the view to the sky.

GENTLE MONSTER

This site is located on the northern side of Dosan Park, and faces back alleys and small commercial buildings on the other side. When a site is surrounded by busy shops and popular restaurants, it is important to design buildings that interact with the street, as well as create a sense of shelter from the hustle and bustle outside.

Towards the south of the park are Maison Southcape (2020; ill. p. 90), another project I designed, and AMORE Sulwhasoo Flagship Store (2016) by Neri & Hu, both projects that create a space where the city can pause. Maison Southcape is a renovation project for a flagship store, with bespoke curved glass creating a special shopping experience. It blurs the boundary between inside and out, highlighting the ever-changing play of light, glass and greenery. Distorted views through the curved glass evoke curiosity and privacy. Internally, concrete blocks with a rough, bold texture create a contrast to the soft fabric and intricate designs of the fashion on offer.

This architectural proposal, originally for Queenmama Market, began with a simple concrete box supporting a smaller gable roof volume perched slightly above the structure. This contrast is a response to the unbalanced surroundings. The main box is covered with horizontal concrete bricks and is raised from the ground to allow for sufficient natural light and air circulation. The greenery of the garden at the entrance continues inside, connecting inside and out. The space was planned as a cultural venue for arts and fashion, and designed to be versatile. Visitors are guided from the ground floor to the top, which forms an inviting open space from street level. This space can be transformed into a café, restaurant, or exhibition hall as required. The top floor is a wire-suspended box,

opposite, above Offset masses with special top floor. At ground level, the garden connects to the street.

overleaf Looking through the curved glass of Maison Southcape.

which allows the ground and first floors enough height to function as a kitchen and hall. The gable roof of the top floor is also reinforced to support later additions for various events.

The three-storey square box is covered with long, narrow concrete bricks, which give a visual sense of materiality and a perceptual depth to the façade, and supporting walls are finished in simple concrete. The gable roof volume is clad with cedar boards, spaced out slightly to allow light to penetrate through the gaps. Cedar boards are intentionally placed outside of the glass to protect from heat gain through the sun, as well as to achieve a simpler, more primitive appearance.

MK MIXED-USE OFFICE BUILDING

The MK building is located in the heart of Gangnam's commercial district, with its many bars and restaurants. It is a shared office building on the fifth to the twelfth floors, with some spaces dedicated for multi-use. The lower levels house facilities such as bars and restaurants. A 3 m (10 ft)-wide walkway through the long, narrow plot allows pedestrians to walk through, connecting the two interior hallways to either side, east and west. The pathway creates a new alley with reflective surfaces and a wall of greenery on one side to increase permeability and pedestrian flow.

To create this large opening on the ground floor, which makes the building appear as if it is resting on one leg, a Y-shaped column was introduced, expressed internally on the upper ten levels. It transfers the load of the building to defined points on the ground. The main circulation core is at the west end of the plot, making it possible for the east to be opened up with views over Gangnam, where the Y-shaped column can be seen from the outside via large openings. Inside, the space is divided up into smaller, box-like areas to allow for a homogeneous and continuous network that is flexible and adaptive. Additional intermediate stairs connecting these spaces at various points evoke a more experiential way of using the building.

To maximize the height of the ceiling, a new type of reinforced ribbed concrete slab with an especially shallow depth was developed. The main supply and extract services run along the perimeter in a recessed section of the slab, partially disguised and almost invisible from the outside. The façade is broken up into smaller, rectangular glass openings, framed in concrete, revealing the language of inserted boxes. A perforated metal screen partially allows transparency, but also provides a degree of shade with a sense of enclosure. The top of the building is visually defined and is home to a roof terrace. With the elements of the passage, fragmented boxes, large folding windows and an open staircase to the lower floors, the architecture sets out to add excitement and a dynamic character to the area.

강
남
구

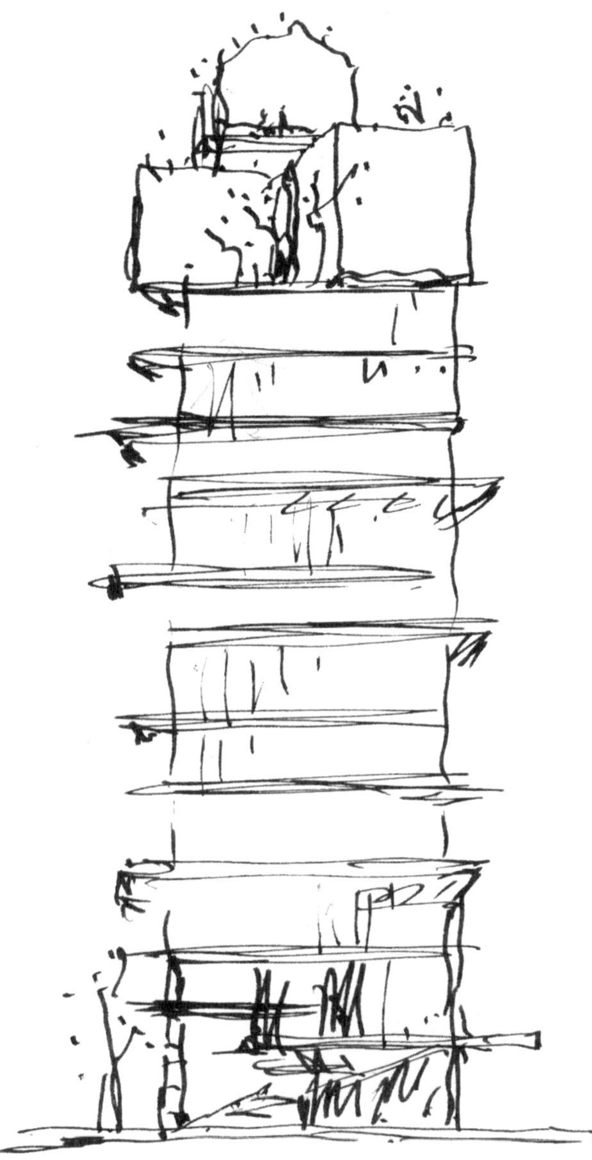

Passage connecting the back alley and main street to either side of the building. When seated in the restaurant area, diners have a view of the extensive bamboo wall opposite.

YANGPYEONG AND NAMYANGJU

Yangpyeong and Namyangju are located in the eastern section of Gyeonggi province, on the outskirts of Seoul. Namyangju connects directly to the city, bordered by the Han River to the south and the Bukhan River to the east. Yangpyeong, southeast of Namyangju, is also on the Han River.

There are no factories or other evidence of industry to disrupt the landscape, which is populated with restaurants, cafés and holiday homes. It is the perfect place for those who live in Seoul, but want to escape the city from time to time. Previously, the land was used for agriculture, but since Seoul's population explosion in the 1980s and '90s, along with the dramatic increase in cars, demand for escaping the city has grown. The change from a six-day to a five-day working week further accelerated this demand by providing more free time to people for recreation and leisure, including me.

I first explored the area when I was invited to design a residential project for a client. When I arrived, it was spring and there was a drizzle trickling down from the clouds. The light was soft and as I was driving my car, the beautiful scenery of rivers, green fields and mountains revealed itself to me. Having this peaceful, natural place so close to the city filled me with joy, and it became somewhere I would often find myself. Soon after that first experience, I had several opportunities to design projects in Yangpyeong, and each time it has been a pleasure to discover more of the area. I especially value the quiet mornings, when the world is slowly waking up. There are no cars to disrupt the silence, and

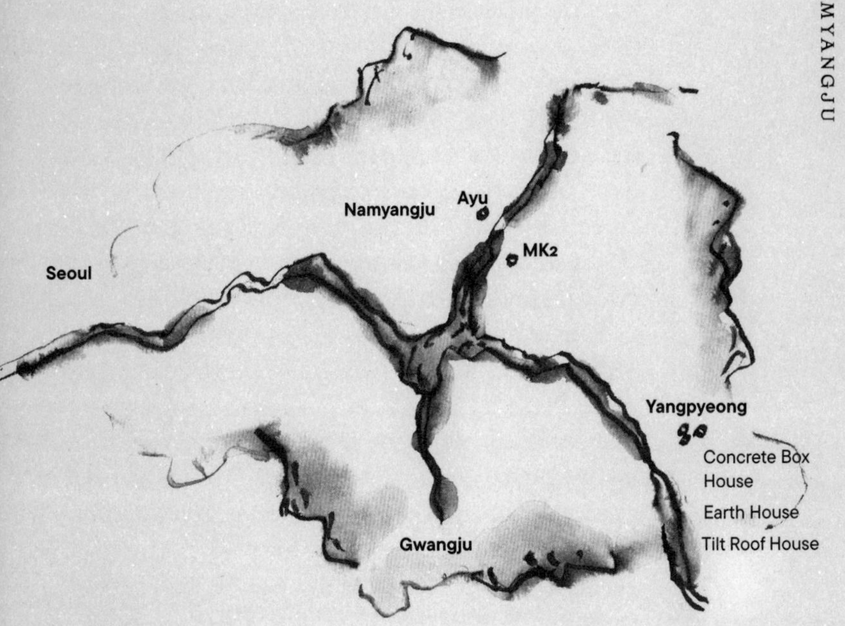
Ayu
Namyangju
MK2
Seoul
Yangpyeong
Concrete Box
House
Earth House
Tilt Roof House
Gwangju

a gentle fog occasionally hovers in the valleys. By listening closely, the sound of rivers and streams can be heard, passing stones and granite rocks on their long journey to the sea. This, together with the sounds of the wind rushing through trees and the birds singing, calms the senses. As my life became hectic in my forties and fifties, these pleasurable moments became very important to me.

Concrete Box House (p. 98) and Earth House (p. 104) were built at about the same time for similar purposes. Concrete Box House was built as a retreat for myself and for people in my office to use as a place for gathering and relaxing, and to serve as a forum for discussions and exhibitions. Earth House is dedicated to the poet Yoon Dong-ju, and the idea for it was based on my reflections when reading and studying his poems. The houses gave me the chance to examine my interest in architecture, and to follow my creative aspirations since I was my own client for both projects. To fully embrace nature in the most dramatic way possible, I went beyond creating an open floorplan on the ground floor. Instead, I focused on creating a few limited openings that would reveal the landscape gradually, which gave each opening a greater meaning. The shape of the buildings are bold, rejecting more complex forms and reading from the outside in.

With this approach, I hoped to achieve the raw experiential and intuitive qualities that I believe are achieved by simple strategic design principles. These qualities are deeply rooted in my own experiences. I try constantly to understand this relationship and how our surroundings influence our minds, especially after reading Mark Twain's short story, 'What is Man?' (1906) as a teenager.

Years after reading the story for the first time, I have finally reached my answer: 'human love'. In my view, Twain misses out on this crucial point, even though love is such a beautiful part of our lives. I also learned that love comes from intuition and emotion, and is not bound to rational logic. This idea is linked back to my principles of architecture. As love cannot be controlled, architecture shall not be fully controlled. There should always be room for the unexpected, since the world is no narrow illusion.

CONCRETE BOX HOUSE

Concrete Box House was designed as a retreat from busy city life, and is located on a peaceful site perched on a hill overlooking the quiet rice fields of Yangpyoung. The design started with a 14 m^2 (151 sq ft) box, and placed a 5 m^2 (54 sq ft) hole in the centre. I feel that designing with the primitive in mind brings mystery back into our lives, both allowing and amplifying our experience of the subtle changes in nature.

I wanted the presence of the moon and moonlight to be strongly felt, and I designed the interior to be a moon-watching space. I intended to draw on my experiences as a child, when I was so intuitively connected to my surroundings. I would watch the moonlight in my room at night as it passed through the large openings of the *hanok* in which I grew up. The design aim was to create a building that would appear quiet and unassuming on the outside, but would engage people with nature on the interior.

This project was the first to provide me with an opportunity to explore my interest in architecture, and is a continuation of my thesis at Harvard, 'Experience and Perception'. Back then, the idea was born from the concept of yin and yang, which thereafter developed into my reflections on intuition, rationality and love. Ever since first reading Twain's story 'What is Man?', I have been drawn to the question of whether true love exists. In the story, the character of the wise old man suggests that what we perceive as love is actually rooted in our own ego, and therefore unconditional love cannot exist. Twain tries to understand his relationship with love, explaining it in a logical and rational manner. He sees love as something that is guided by the calculated decisions we make in life to find our own happiness. This suggests that humans would not do something unless it was beneficial to them.

When I watched the plot-twisting final scene of the Netflix series *Squid Game*, I was reminded of this concept. For me, it shows that human relationships and the empathy we feel for one another are far more multidimensional. Human behaviour and feelings cannot be explained with words in a general scenario. In the final scene, a man is

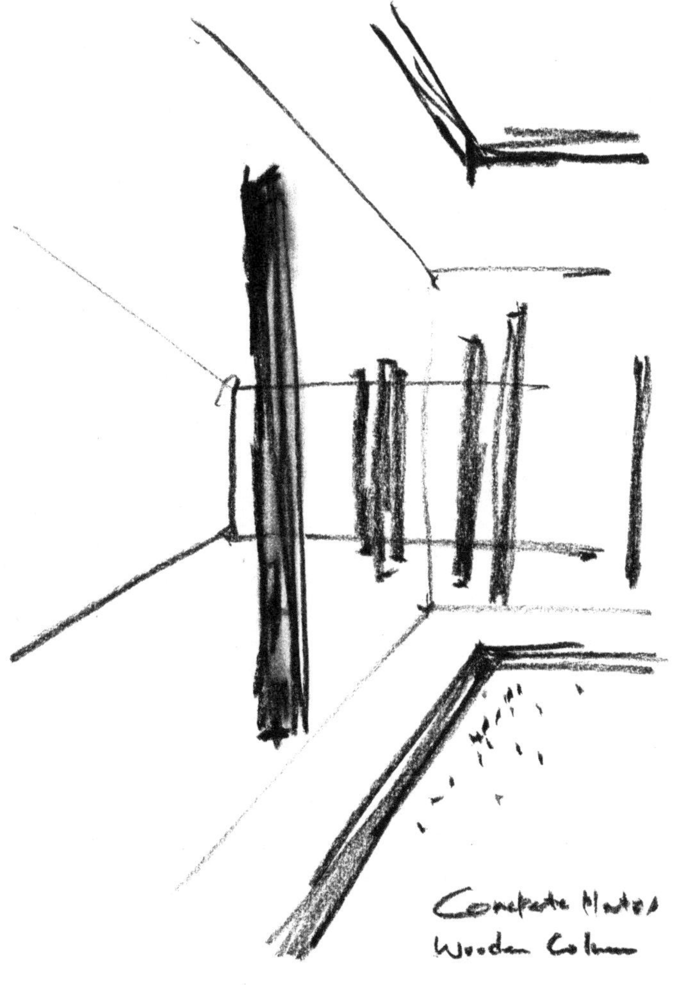
Concrete Plates
Wooden Column

양평 남양주

above The simple shape contrasts with Concrete Box House's organic surroundings, but is still part of nature.

overleaf The courtyard opens up to the sky, with the ceiling supported by wooden columns.

destined to sleep on the street on a snowy day, and may perish from the cold. At first, his situation seems helpless. The character Oh Il-nam (played by O Yeong-su), observing the situation from afar, states that no one will save the man from freezing to death and starvation. People are too self-centred and busy with their own lives. During Oh Il-nam's final moments, however, an ambulance arrives to save the man on the street. *Squid Game* touches on many questions about human behaviour and evolutionary psychology. By building up a tense narrative with twists and turns, viewers automatically reflect on their own feelings about how people live as a community of individuals. When I watched the show, I thought that the director must have read Twain's story. The parallels between the attitudes to the life of the wise old man and Oh Il-nam are clear. They both have a bitter relationship with humankind, perhaps influenced by bad experiences in their lives.

It took me over a decade to conclude that emotion and love are the truths that make life beautiful. I was too distracted by other noise before that. As a student, I aspired to learn more about architecture that is derived from emotion and intuition, rather than one that is solely guided by logic. When I was in my early thirties, I became a father. My daughter Suehyan was born first, with Sueminn following in 1991, right in the middle of my thesis studies at Harvard. Finally, my youngest daughter Suea was born. By this time I had returned to Korea and was working very hard to survive as a young architect.

Before becoming a father, my perception of architecture was only based on my academic studies. But the compassion I learned from becoming a father was vital during my journey of discovering my purpose within the profession I chose. This sense of care and affection trickled into my thesis. It was something I often felt was missing. I am convinced that if you look closely enough, it is all around us, like the care demonstrated in the final scene of *Squid Game*: the serendipitous act of giving help by one stranger to another in need.

EARTH HOUSE

I further explored the principles first investigated in Concrete Box House with Earth House, which was built in honour of the Korean poet Yoon Dong-ju. Just as his poetry expresses hope for the future in times of great threat – which he tried to achieve through self-restraint and self-reflection – my hope is that this building will be a home in which one can reflect and feel present.

Like Concrete Box House, Earth House focuses on the primal relationship between nature and humans. It is built with careful consideration for constructional efficiency, but also responds to our somatic senses. In my work, I try to explore human sentiment by creating a connection between earth and sky, rain and snow, sunlight and moonlight, stillness and wind, silence and the mellow sound that bounces off the surfaces of a minimally designed space.

The house is small, 14 × 7 m (46 × 23 ft), and is buried in the ground. It contains six 1-*pyeong* rooms and a courtyard, which opens up to the sky. One *pyeong* is a little over 3 m^2 (32 sq ft), so the rooms are just big enough for an adult to lie down flat; they can also be connected to form one large space. There is a small kitchen, a study, two WCs, a bathroom with a wooden tub and toilet, and a washroom. The doors are small, and entering the house requires contorting one's body into a smaller shape.

The lateral pressure from the earth on all four sides is resisted by thick concrete retaining walls and a flat roof. The rammed earth used for the walls was obtained from the excavation of the site. A combination of passive cooling and geothermal tubes buried in the earth around the house keep the temperature cool in summer and warm in winter. A pine tree that had to be taken down was cut into 80 mm (3 in.)-thick slices, and then cast into the concrete walls of the courtyard. As the slices decay, they will host smaller plants and new life will begin. All of the interior furniture is recycled wood from old Korean gates.

Stairs lead down to the entrance in the foreground.

TILT ROOF HOUSE

The natural lines of the ground are very interesting to me. I see the groundscape as very powerful, like the Nazca lines in Peru, or Richard Long's lines made by walking, Mary Callery's abstract sculptures and the land art of Michael Heizer. I am also very interested in Taoism and the ideas of yin and yang. The *Tao Te Ching* states: 'Earth is never born, so never living; it does not have life itself, but gives life'.

To me, the earth is very calm and poetic, and deeply entrenched in the notions of life and death. The design for Tilt Roof House stemmed from this admiration for the organic rhythms and properties of the earth. It cuts negative forms into the roof that penetrate down into the building mass, which in turn makes positive forms on the ceiling from the inside.

overleaf View down the hill to Tilt Roof House, with its recessed areas for outdoor seating.

The tilt of the roof follows the slope of the ground. By lowering two of the roof squares down into the building, one about 45 cm (18 in.) and the other 60 cm (24 in.), the receded spaces feel very comfortable when seated inside. The roof space also became important because there was not much ground space available. In a way, it became a substitute for the ground. The third square is an open courtyard that goes down to ground level, which allows air and light to penetrate into the house. The two lowered squares from the roof continue into the space below, where they are visible as positive forms, and function as lowered ceilings in the kitchen and bedroom. This effect is also used in the lowering of the ground level in the bedroom.

I'm fascinated by the relationship between the human body and the experience of the plane. For instance, when your body is approximately 60 cm (24 in.) below the surface, your awareness of the ground becomes much stronger. I experienced this on a hill, where I found a hole from a removed tree – I sat in it and instantly felt comfortable. When I talk about 'experience and perception', this is what I mean. Sometimes small gestures evoke a big emotional response. In my projects, that is what I strive constantly to achieve.

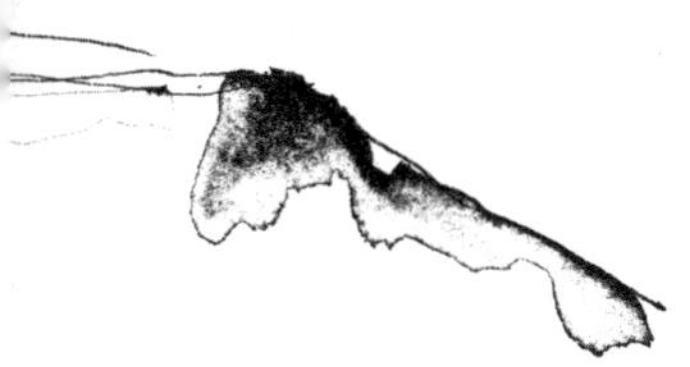

MK2 FURNITURE GALLERY

The clients for this project are my friends and neighbours from the Seochon area, a couple who are also artists, furniture dealers and designers. They wanted a home and gallery in Seojong, where they could afford a larger space. Other friends of theirs also own galleries in the area, and there is a community of like-minded people who have created a relaxed yet inspiring atmosphere with creative work and many places to discover.

Along the Bukhangang, galleries, cafés, restaurants and retreat houses began popping up earlier than in the Yangpyeong area of the Namhangang. Today, the area is very busy, with many buildings built in the last twenty years or so. The site for this project is located in the middle of this chaotic context, so I thought that the design should be simple yet bold, making a statement without demanding too much attention.

The MK2 Furniture Gallery serves as a multifunctional space that acts as a showcase, residence and storage for the couple, who are relocating from the centre of Seoul to the suburbs. The lower levels of the building are planned as a single, undisturbed space that provides flexibility for art storage and exhibitions. Surrounded by a disorganized array of random buildings, the ground level is in keeping with its exterior, punctured occasionally by large windows, but kept simple in the form of a monolithic concrete façade. As the building triangulates upwards, the rooftop residence has slits and openings oriented to the sky, which provide ample daylight, ventilation and semi-private views to the surrounding neighbourhood.

MK 2
Solid shell
for the soft organic
nature of light &
breeze

AYU SPACE

AYU Space was designed with multiple purposes in mind, which could be embraced within the overall idea of displaying art and hosting a café. The setting, located along the Bukhangang with a view of the mountains on the other side, makes this place unique. The Bukhangang is a tributary of the Han River, which flows through North and South Korea, traversing Kangwon province in the north and Gangwon and Gyeonggi provinces in the south. In Korean culture, the connection to rivers is very important. There are several mountains, and therefore many rivers. Because of the granite rocks and rocky riverbeds, the water is very clear and people used to drink it straight from the river without having to boil it first. This is yet another example of why the connection to the landscape is so significant.

Two existing buildings and a few noteworthy trees dominated the site before the new addition was placed. From the earliest design stages, I thought it was important to embrace all of these existing features, as they gave the site its character. In a way, the new building was a means to knit the various elements of the site together, and to unite them in a place where visitors would be able to experience the interplay of rivers and mountains, with the existing *hanok* and ginkgo tree.

When visitors enter the main building, their gaze follows the slope of the terrain through the large windows to the river in the south. The farthest window enters the building and approaches the courtyard, where glimpses of the mountains to the east and the ginkgo tree can be seen. The interior space around the elliptical courtyard allows visitors to sit on tiered seating in pocket-like areas to enjoy the space and the views. Depending on the natural features of the site and the topography, the roof slopes up and down. It does not attempt to form a perfect ellipse, but frames the views while resting softly against the natural backdrop. This approach is further amplified by an entry wall that extends to the outside, embracing the existing *hanok* and leading visitors into the gallery space.

Ayu Space

when River, hills,
Ginkgo tree flows in..

Next to the new main building is an existing residential building from the 1970s and ’80s. To ease the view that was once dominated by the strong structural language of the existing building and the presence of a large bridge, the adaptive reuse of the space adds stainless-steel frames to create a new enclosure while opening up the space visually to the south. The materials blend into the surroundings by reflecting the water and sky. The rear of the building is kept solid as it was, but inside a folded plywood shell has been added along the west wall to further direct the focus of attention to the river.

View from the top of AYU looking into the courtyard and interior spaces with the undulating roof surface tying into the landscape.

CONCLUSION

My life as an architect in Seoul has been a mission because of high expectations, yet it has been a very happy journey, becoming richer and more meaningful as I pursued my career. It is a city in which society and daily life have undergone rapid change and development. While living here, I have seen the streetscape change, buildings grow taller, streets become wider, and neon lights start to creep across the façades of buildings. I have also noticed a shift in the behaviour of the people who live here. In my childhood, I enjoyed watching people playing games outside or groups of people gathering at street corners to chat. Now, you need to be careful to avoid walking into someone looking down at their phone or rushing off to the next appointment, and many more cars fill the streets.

Life in Seoul has become more fast-paced and has lost its intimacy in some areas. Yet it is also a city that is filled with opportunities, testament to Seoul's vitality and ability to adapt to changing conditions. Something powerful is lingering beneath the surface. There is a critical mass of creative people here, and I am very thankful to those I have had the opportunity to work with, from clients, consultants and builders to the young people in my office, some from Korea and some from elsewhere. After over thirty years of practice as an architect, I realize people are everything: happiness and memories.

DIRECTORY

'–' Shaped Studio Residence [p. 50]
475-35 Pyeongchang-dong, Jongno-gu, Seoul 03004

A By Bom [pp. 84–5]
91-3 Cheongdam-dong, Gangnam-gu, Seoul 06016
abybomcos.com

AMORE Sulwhasoo Flagship Store [p. 88]
650 Sinsa-dong, Gangnam-gu, Seoul 06021
sulwhasoo.com/kr/ko/flagship/dosan

Art Museum of Park No-Su [p. 36]
168-2 Ogin-dong, Jongno-gu, Seoul 03034
jfac.or.kr/site/main/content/parkns01

Arumjigi Building [p. 36]
35-32 Tongui-dong, Jongno-gu, Seoul 03044
arumjigi.org

AYU Space [pp. 112–14]
445-21, Geumnam-ri, Hwado-eup, Namyangju-si, Gyeonggi-do 472842
ayuspace.kr

BE-Twixt [pp. 78–80]
92-13, Cheongdam-dong, Gangnam-gu, Seoul 06016

Biwon Secret Garden [p. 26]
2-71 Waryong-dong, Jongno-gu, Seoul 03072
cdg.go.kr

Boutique Monaco: Missing Matrix [p. 76]
1316-5 Seocho-dong, Seocho-gu, Seoul 06616
boutiquemonaco.co.kr

Buam House [p. 56]
319-4 Buam-dong, Jongno-gu, Seoul 03022

Café Onion Seongsu [p. 65]
277-135 Seongsu-dong 2(i)-ga, Seongdong-gu, Seoul 04797
onionkr.com

Changamjang Residence [p. 51]
449-2 Pyeongchang-dong, Jongno-gu, Seoul 03004

Changdeok Palace [p. 26]
2-71 Waryong-dong, Jongno-gu, Seoul 03072
cdg.go.kr

Changuimun Gate [p. 57]
248 Buam-dong, Jongno-gu, Seoul 03020

Chungha Building [p. 71]
100-32 Cheongdam-dong, Gangnam-gu, Seoul 06010

Concrete Box House [pp. 98–103]
789-3, Sugok-ri, Jipyeong-myeon, Yangpyeong-gun, Gyeonggi-do 12544

Daelim Warehouse [p. 65]
322-32 Seongsu-dong 2(i)-ga, Seongdong-gu, Seoul 04784
instagram.com/daelimchanggo_gallery

Dior Boutique [p. 71]
98-3 Cheongdam-dong, Gangnam-gu, Seoul 06015
dior.com

Dongshipjagak Gate [p. 22]
20 Dosan-daero 45-gil, Sinsa-dong, Gangnam, Seoul 03045

Dosan Park [p. 88]
1-58 Sejongno, Jongno-gu, Seoul 03045

Earth House [pp. 104–5]
789-55 Sugok-ri, Jipyeong-myeon, Yangpyeong-gun, Gyeonggi-do 12544

ECS (Eatery Culture Seongsu) [pp. 68–9]
271-12, Seongsu-dong 2(i)-ga, Seongdong-gu, Seoul 133120

E-Shaped House [p. 61]
135-41 Itaewon-dong, Yongsan-gu, Seoul 04349

Four Box House [p. 50]
438-11 Pyeongchang-dong, Jongno-gu, Seoul 03003

4th Seoul Biennale of Architecture and Urbanism [pp. 32–3]
48-9, Songhyeon-dong, Jongno-gu, Seoul 11018

Freedom Centre [p. 12]
201-6 Jangchung-dong
2(i)-ga, Jung-gu,
Seoul 04605

Galleria Department
Store [p. 70]
494 Apgujeong-dong,
Gangnam-gu,
Seoul 06008
dept.galleria.co.kr

Gana Art Centre [p. 52]
97 Pyeongchang-dong,
Jongno-gu, Seoul 03004
ganaart.com

Gangnam Station
[p. 71]
858 Yeoksam-dong,
Gangnam-gu,
Seoul 06232

Gentle Monster
[pp. 88–90]
649-8 Sinsa-dong,
Gangnam-gu,
Seoul 06020

GIZI Exhibition and
Residence [pp. 48–9]
79-22 Yeonhui-dong,
Seodaemun-gu,
Seoul 03723

Gugidong House [p. 50]
226-37 Gugi-dong,
Jongno-gu, Seoul 03000

Gyeongbokgung Palace
[pp. 20–1]
1-1 Sejongno, Jongno-
gu, Seoul 03045
royalpalace.go.kr

Gyeongbokgung
Station [p. 34]
81-1 Jeokseon-dong,
Jongno-gu, Seoul 03170

Gyeonghoeru Pavilion
[p. 16]
37, Samcheong-ro,
Jongno-gu, Seoul

Hangangjin Station
[p. 61]
726-494 Hannam-dong,
Yongsan-gu,
Seoul 04347

Hannam-dong Office
[pp. 62–3]
657-42 Hannam-dong,
Yongsan-gu,
Seoul 04401

Hyundai Card Music
Library [p. 61]
683-132 Hannam-dong,
Yongsan-gu,
Seoul 04400
dive.hyundaicard.com/
web/musiclibrary

Jongmyo Royal Shrine
[p. 26]
1-2 Hunjeong-dong,
Jongno-gu, Seoul 03135
jm.cha.go.kr

Jongno Tower [p. 27]
6 Jongno 2(i)-ga,
Jongno-gu, Seoul 03161

Kim Chong Yung
Museum [p. 52]
114-8 Pyeongchang-
dong, Jongno-gu,
Seoul 03004
kimchongyung.com

Kukje Gallery [p. 27]
48 Sogyeok-dong,
Jongno-gu, Seoul 03053
kukjegallery.com

Kyobo Tower [p. 73]
1303-22 Seocho-dong,
Seocho-gu, Seoul 06611
kyobobook.co.kr/
store/?storeCode=015

Kyungdong
Presbyterian Church
[p. 12]
26-6 Jangchung-dong
1(il)-ga, Jung-gu,
Seoul 04614
kdchurch.or.kr

Leeum Samsung
Museum of Art [p. 61]
742-1 Hannam-dong,
Yongsan-gu,
Seoul 04348
leeum.org

Lotte World Tower
[p. 64]
29 Sincheon-dong,
Songpa-gu, Seoul 05551
lwt.co.kr/ko/main/
main.do

Louis Vuitton Maison
[p. 71]
99-18 Cheongdam-
dong, Gangnam-gu,
Seoul 06015
kr.louisvuitton.com/
kor-kr/art/maison-
seoul

Maison Southcape
[p. 88]
631-34 Sinsa-dong,
Gangnam-gu,
Seoul 06021

MK Mixed-use Office
Building [pp. 91–3]
1308-7 Seocho-dong,
Seocho-gu, Seoul 06612

MK2 Furniture Gallery
[pp. 110–11]
779-14 Munho-ri,
Seojong-myeon,
Yangpyeong-gun,
Gyeonggi-do 12503

Namsan Tower [p. 60]
1-3 Yongsan-dong 2(i)-ga, Yongsan-gu,
Seoul 04340
seoultower.co.kr

National Museum of Modern and Contemporary Art [p. 27]
165 Sogyeok-dong, Jongno-gu, Seoul 03062
mmca.go.kr/eng

National Theatre [p. 16]
14-67 Jangchung-dong 2(i)-ga, Jung-gu,
Seoul 04621
ntok.go.kr/en

Onground Café Gallery [pp. 42–6]
23 Jahamun-ro 10-gil, Jongno-gu, Seoul 03043

Onjium [p. 36]
17-1 Changseong-dong, Jongno-gu, Seoul 03043
onjium.org

Pace Gallery [p. 61]
740-1 Hannam-dong, Yongsan-gu,
Seoul 04348
pacegallery.com

Patema Inverted [p. 65]
286-19 Haengdang-dong, Seongdong-gu,
Seoul 04715

Project Space Mahk [pp. 38–41]
85-1 Tongui-dong, Jongno-gu, Seoul 03044

Queenmama Market [p. 88]
50 Apgujeong-ro 46-gil, Gangnam-gu, Seoul
queenmamamarket.com

Ramp Building [pp. 81–3]
1652-420 Beopheung-ri, Tanhyeon-myeon, Paju-si,
Gyeonggi-do 10859

Seokpajeong Seoul Art Museum [p. 57]
201 Buam-dong, Jongno-gu, Seoul 03021
seoulmuseum.org

Seongsu WAVE Commercial Building [p. 65]
668-70 Seongsu-dong 1(il)-ga, Seongdong-gu,
Seoul 04768

Seoul Forest Park [p. 64]
273 Ttukseom-ro, Seongdong-gu, Seoul

Seoul New City Hall [p. 27]
31 Taepyeongno 1(il)-ga, Jung-gu, Seoul 04524
seoul.go.kr/main/index.jsp

Songwon Art Centre [p. 27]
106-5 Hwa-dong, Jongno-gu, Seoul 03061
songwonart.org

Sounds Hannam [p. 62]
657-128 Hannam-dong, Yongsan-gu,
Seoul 04401
instagram.com/sounds.hannam

Space Group Building [p. 12]
128-6 Pildong 2(i)-ga, Jung-gu, Seoul 04626

Starfield COEX Mall [p. 71]
159 Samseong-dong, Gangnam-gu,
Seoul 06164
starfield.co.kr/coexmall/main.do

ST SongEun Building [p. 80]
92-9 Cheongdam-dong, Gangnam-gu,
Seoul 06016

Thaddaeus Ropac [p. 61]
1-90 Hannam-dong, Yongsan-gu,
Seoul 04420
ropac.net

Theground Music and Art Studio [pp. 47]
10-15 Jahamun-ro 12-gil, Jongno-gu, Seoul 03043

Tilt Roof House [pp. 106–9]
Jipyeong-myeon, Yangpyeong-gun,
Gyeonggi-do

Tongin Market [p. 34]
10-3 Tongin-dong, Jongno-gu, Seoul 03036
tonginmarket.modoo.at

Total Museum [p. 51]
465-16 Pyeongchang-dong, Jongno-gu,
Seoul 03004
totalmuseum.org

Tower Hotel [p. 12]
201 Jangchung-dong 2(i)-ga, Jung-gu,
Seoul 04605

Twin Trees [p. 22–5]
14 Junghak-dong, Jongno-gu, Seoul 03142

Urban Hive [p. 73]
200-7 Nonhyeon-dong,
Gangnam-gu,
Seoul 06120

Welcomm City [p. 19]
190-10 Jangchung-dong
2(i)-ga, Jung-gu,
Seoul 04617

Whanki Museum [p. 57]
210-8 Buam-dong,
Jongno-gu, Seoul 03020
whankimuseum.org

W Mission (interior
design) [p. 64]
656-1206 Seongsu-dong
1(il)-ga, Seongdong-gu,
Seoul 04779

Wooran Foundation
[p. 66]
314-12 Seongsu-dong
2(i)-ga, Seongdong-gu,
Seoul 04782

Yeol Gallery [pp. 30–1]
177-7 Gahoe-dong,
Jongno-gu, Seoul 03056

Yoon Dong-ju
Literature Museum
[p. 57]
3-100 Cheongun-dong,
Jongno-gu, Seoul 03046
jfac.or.kr/site/main/
content/yoondj01

BUILDINGS BY BCHO ARCHITECTS

'–' Shaped Studio
Residence [p. 50]
Area: 418 m^2
(4,499 sq ft)
Completed: 1997

A By Bom [pp. 84–5]
Area: 3,000 m^2
(32,292 sq ft)
Completed: 2021

AYU Space [pp. 112–14]
Area: 1,401 m^2
(15,080 sq ft)
Completed: 2023
(expected)

BE-Twixt [pp. 78–80]
Area: 1,665 m^2
(17,922 sq ft)
Completed: 2007

Buam House [p. 56]
Area: 45 m^2 (484 sq ft)
Completed: 2020

Concrete Box House
[pp. 98–103]
Area: 191 m^2 (2,057 sq ft)
Completed: 2004

Earth House [pp. 104–5]
Area: 32 m^2 (344 sq ft)
Completed: 2009

ECS (Eatery Culture
Seongsu) [pp. 68–9]
Area: 1,675 m^2
(18,030 sq ft)
Completed: 2023
(expected)

E-Shaped House [p. 61]
Area: 985 m^2
(10,603 sq ft)
Completed: 2008

Four Box House [p. 50]
Area: 133 m^2 (1,432 sq ft)
Completed: 2007

4th Seoul Biennale
of Architecture and
Urbanism [pp. 32–3]
Area: 45,000 m^2
(484,376 sq ft)
Completed: 2023
(expected)

Gentle Monster
[pp. 88–90]
Area: 2,372 m^2
(25,532 sq ft)
Completed: 2015

GIZI Exhibition and
Residence [pp. 48–9]
Area: 1,997 m^2
(21,496 sq ft)
Completed: 2018

Gugidong House [p. 50]
Area: 276 m^2 (2,971 sq ft)
Completed: 2018

Hannam-dong Office
[pp. 62–3]
Area: 488 m^2
(5,253 sq ft)
Completed: 2018

Maison Southcape
[p. 88]
Area: 2,133 m^2
(22,959 sq ft)
Completed: 2020

MK Mixed-use Office
Building [pp. 91–3]
Area: 2,670 m^2
(28,740 sq ft)
Completed: 2022

MK2 Furniture Gallery
[pp. 110–11]
Area: 475 m^2 (5,113 sq ft)
Completed: 2020

Onground Café Gallery [pp. 42–6]
Area: 62 m² (667 sq ft)
Completed: 2020

Project Space Mahk [pp. 38–41]
Area: 139 m² (1,496 sq ft)
Completed: 2021

Ramp Building [pp. 81–3]
Area: 231 m² (2,486 sq ft)
Completed: 2004

Theground Music and Art Studio [pp. 47]
Area: 436 m² (4,693 sq ft)
Completed: 2017

Tilt Roof House [pp. 106–9]
Area: 162 m² (1,744 sq ft)
Completed: 2014

Twin Trees [pp. 22–5]
Area: 54,919 m² (591,143 sq ft)
Completed: 2010

W Mission (interior design) [p. 64]
Area: 9,101 m² (97,962 sq ft)
Completed: 2023

Yeol Gallery [pp. 30–1]
Area: 2,734 m² (29,429 sq ft)
Completed: 2017

BUILDINGS BY OTHER ARCHITECTS

AMORE Sulwhasoo Flagship Store [p. 88]
Architect: Neri & Hu Design and Research Office
Completed: 2016

Art Museum of Park No-Su [p. 36]
Architect: Park Gil-ryong
Completed: 1937

Arumjigi Building [p. 36]
Architect: Kim Jongkyu
Completed: 2013

Boutique Monaco: Missing Matrix [p. 76]
Architect: Mass Studies
Completed: 2008

Changamjang Residence [p. 51]
Architect: Kim Swoo-geun
Completed: 1974

Chungha Building [p. 71]
Architect: MVRDV
Completed: 2013

Dior Boutique [p. 71]
Architect: Christian de Portzamparc, Peter Marino
Completed: 2015

Freedom Centre [p. 12]
Architect: Kim Swoo-geun
Completed: 1963

Galleria Department Store [p. 70]
Architect: UN Studio
Completed: 2004

Gana Art Centre [p. 52]
Architect: Wilmotte & Associés, Total Design
Completed: 1998

Hyundai Card Music Library [p. 61]
Architect: Choi Moongyu
Completed: 2015

Jongno Tower [p. 27]
Architect: Rafael Viñoly Architects
Completed: 1999

Kim Chong Yung Museum [p. 52]
Architect: Poetry Architecture
Completed: 2002

Kukje Gallery [p. 27]
Architect: SO-IL
Completed: 2012

Kyobo Tower [p. 73]
Architect: Mario Botta
Completed: 2003

Kyungdong Presbyterian Church [p. 12]
Architect: Kim Swoo-geun
Completed: 1980

Leeum Samsung Museum of Art [p. 61]
Architect: Mario Botta, Jean Nouvel and Rem Koolhaas
Completed: 2004

Louis Vuitton Maison [p. 71]
Architect: Frank Gehry
Completed: 2019

National Museum of Modern and Contemporary Art [p. 27]
Architect: MPART Architects
Completed: 2013

National Theatre [p. 16]
Architect: Lee Hee-tae
Completed: 1973

Onjium [p. 36]
Architect: One O One Architects
Completed: 2018

Pace Gallery [p. 61]
Architect: Mass Studies
Completed: 2022

Patema Inverted [p. 65]
Architect: L'EAU design
Completed: 2020

Seongsu WAVE Commercial Building [p. 65]
Architect: JYA-Rchitects
Completed: 2022

Seoul New City Hall [p. 27]
Architect: IARC Architects
Completed: 2013

Songwon Art Centre [p. 27]
Architect: Mass Studies
Completed: 2012

Space Group Building [p. 12]
Architect: Kim Swoo-geun
Completed: 1971

ST SongEun Building [p. 80]
Architect: Herzog & de Meuron
Completed: 2021

Total Museum [p. 51]
Architect: Shin-Kyu Moon
Completed: 1984

Tower Hotel [p. 12]
Architect: Kim Swoo-geun
Completed: 1969

Urban Hive [p. 73]
Architect: Archium
Completed: 2008

Welcomm City [p. 19]
Architect: Seung H-Sang
Completed: 2000

Whanki Museum [p. 57]
Architect: Kyu-seung Woo
Completed: 1992

Wooran Foundation [p. 66]
Architect: System Lab
Completed: 2018

Yoon Dong-ju Literature Museum [p. 57]
Architect: Lee So-jin
Completed: 2012

ACKNOWLEDGMENTS

Seoul is a big city to put together in a small book, but I tried to select and introduce some key areas with different characteristics to help readers grasp the essence of Seoul, along with some background information about the overall composition and development of the city. I wanted to share my personal experience of Seoul with visitors who will visit in the future. I hope that this little book will function as a guide to discovering the city and to understanding my architectural projects in terms of how they relate to their surroundings and my architectural philosophy.

I would like to express my gratitude to Lucas Dietrich, Augusta Pownall and the team at Thames & Hudson. I would also like to extend my appreciation to Fiona Bae, for connecting and assisting me with this publication in London.

The works in these pages were only possible with the help of the people at BCHO Architects, especially my three partners: Jihyun Lee, Kyoungjin Hong and Jayoon Yoon. Special thanks also go to Johanna Kleesattel for putting together the text and materials necessary to realize the book, and for her passionate enthusiasm.

BYOUNG CHO founded BCHO Architects Associates in Seoul, South Korea, in 1994. Over the last three decades, he has built up a reputation as one of the key architects driving the expansion of one of the world's most densely populated cities. Byoung is the general director of the Seoul Biennale of Architecture and Urbanism 2023.

On the cover: Twin Trees (2010), Gangbuk (photo: Young Kwan Kim)

First published in the United Kingdom in 2023 by Thames & Hudson Ltd, 181A High Holborn, London WC1V 7QX

First published in the United States of America in 2023 by Thames & Hudson Inc., 500 Fifth Avenue, New York, New York 10110

British Library Cataloguing-in-Publication Data
A catalogue record for this book is available from the British Library

Library of Congress Control Number 2023939223

ISBN 978-0-500-02711-0

Printed and bound in China by C&C Offset Printing Co. Ltd.